Removing the Obstacles to Effective Leadership

Effective Leadership
Vol. 1

By

Marc Royer Ph.D.

Removing the Obstacles to Effective Leadership
Effective Leadership Volume 1

Copyright 2005
Marc D. Royer
All Rights Reserved

Scripture quotations are taken from the New International Version Copyright 1983, Zondervan Corporation. Used by Permission.

Published by:
The Christian Resource Group
717 Bainbridge Place
Goshen, IN 46526
(574) 533-5133
www.tcrg.org

ISBN 0-9705958-3-2
Library of Congress Control Number: 2004097547

Printed in the United States by Morris Publishing
3212 East Highway 30
Kearney, NE 68847
1-800-650-7888

OTHER BOOKS BY DR. MARC ROYER

Secrets: Exposing, Resolving & Overcoming the Secrets We Carry with Us

Handling Death Dying and Grief

Rejection: Turning You Lemons into Lemonade

Happiness in 30 Days or Less

Financial Freedom Starting Today

Practical Patience

The Development Manual Series

Volume I: A Study in the Old Testament

Volume II: A Study in the New Testament

A Study in the Life of David

A Study in the Prophets

Hell No!

Square Peg, Round Hole

Hocus Focus

The Spiritual Warfare Manual

Go Hard or Go Home

Write:
The Christian Resource Group
717 Bainbridge Place
Goshen, IN 46526

Or visit our web site at www.tcrg.org
Request These Titles from Your Local Bookstore

TABLE OF CONTENTS

REMOVING THE OBSTACLES TO EFFECTIVE LEADERSHIP
INTRODUCTION

- What if your spiritual life was bankrupt **right now** and you didn't even realize it?

- What if you have been fooling everyone so long that you are even **fooling yourself?**

- What i f y ou have b een "spiritualizing" a nd " ministering" so long that **you are empty** on the inside?

- What if you are so blind to your own spiritual need that you couldn't perceive **your own need** even if you wanted to?

The Apostle Paul gives us the warning concerning this potential spiritual condition of Christian leaders when he writes in 1 Corinthians 9:27—**"But I discipline my body and bring** *it* **into s ubjection, l est, when I h ave p reached t o others, I myself should become disqualified."**

How sad the thought is that a Christian leader could spend their entire adult life helping others spiritually but be spiritually bankrupt. Jesus was concerned enough about the possibility that he addressed it in His Sermon on the Mount—(Matthew Chapter 7) **[21]"Not everyone who says to Me, 'Lord, Lord,' shall enter the kingdom of heaven, but he who does the will of My Father in heaven. [22]Many will say to Me in that day, 'Lord, Lord, have we not prophesied in Your name, cast out demons in Your name, and done many wonders in Your name?' [23]And then I w ill declare to t hem, ' I never knew you; depart from Me, you who practice lawlessness!'[24]"Therefore whoever hears these sayings of Mine, and does them, I will liken him to a wise man who** built his house on the rock: [25]and the rain descended, the floods came, and the winds blew and beat on that house; and it did not fall, for it was founded on the rock. [26]"But everyone who hears these sayings of Mine, and does not do them, will be like a foolish man who built his house on the sand: [27]and the rain descended, the floods came, and the winds blew and beat on that house; and it fell. And great was its fall."

BALANCE: The key to effective leadership.

In the same Sermon Jesus also said—[5:48] "Therefore you shall be perfect, just as your Father in heaven is perfect." The Greek word for perfect means "complete" or in our English vernacular "balanced."

"Balance" should be the greatest concern for every Christian leader. The "evil doers" Jesus talks about are those who are unbalanced leaders.

It shouldn't surprise us that God has provided us with the necessary tools in leadership development. This is seen in 1 & 2 Timothy of the New Testament. It is here that the spiritual father, Paul, instructs his "son in the ministry," Timothy.

Through these two letters everyone in Christian ministry must come and sit awhile for careful self-examination. No one should be excluded from this important task.

Contrary to what many believe, ministry is not the most important thing—the reason behind the ministry (the motive) is. Pure ministry not only reaches out to others, but sets the pace of personal holiness and works to remove obstacles to effective leadership we see reiterated to young Timothy by Paul.

> ## *MOTIVE: The WHY is more important than the WHAT.*

This study will unveil eleven specific obstacles for Christian leaders in the development of their leadership.

The focus is not on condemnation but upon revelation—what are the potential pitfalls and how can we deal with them? Further, how can we use a potential obstacle to help develop depth in a Christian leader?

QUESTIONS FOR DISCUSSION

1. Describe a situation when you knew someone who seemed sincere in motive but later found out something different about them. _____

   _____
   _____
   _____
   _____
   _____

2. How do you stay aware of your own motives?

   _____
   _____
   _____
   _____

3. Suggest some ways a Christian leader can stay balanced in his/her life?

   _____
   _____
   _____
   _____
   _____

4. What is the best approach to take in helping people who have become unbalanced without condemning them?

   _____
   _____
   _____
   _____

OBSTACLE #1
The Competitive Spirit

Our natural drives, talents or gifts are a tremendous blessing—or—they can be a tremendous detriment. It all depends upon the motive behind the use of them as well as the attitude in their application. An obstacle develops in leadership when talent and drive becomes misappropriated. It reveals itself through an obvious **competitive spirit**.

The competitive spirit can most obviously be seen in three attitudes:

- Jealousy at the success of others.
- Making excuses for yourself when someone else achieves something better than you.
- Dishonestly representing one.

All three of these attitudes can be neatly packaged and very deceptive. These attitudes can often be almost unrecognizable. They are **"Unrecognizable"** because competition is so accepted by our culture. Compounded by how Christian leaders "spiritualize" competition—the competitive spirit continues to erode away how effective leadership can be.

Anyone involved in church work knows how easy it is to get caught up in numbers. We are directed by leadership how important numbers are. Numbers represent souls—numbers indicate effectiveness—numbers tell the story (and so on).

The truth is numbers have no emotion. They can indicate effectiveness but what the competitive spirit has done is erode common integrity and honesty. What was once a means to an

9

end (reporting effectiveness) has become the main thing. Christian leaders feeling under pressure justify padding their numbers here and there—or exaggerating their effectiveness using numerical statistics because they know how to play what has become a game.

We are still finding out financial and legal the results of corporations who did the same thing through the 1990's to enhance their stockholder prospectuses.

Motivated by greed, corporate officers misreported, misrepresented, and misquoted everything from net worth to expense accounts. The result has become disastrous.

The result in Christian leadership is just as disastrous, but not as obvious until the end.

There are several observations that can be made from what happens when a leader gets caught up in a competitive spirit as it becomes an obstacle of leadership.

1. **Leaders who exaggerate numbers work against the very reason for the numbers.** We report statistics for a written record. If the report is inaccurate, there is really no record. We report statistics for accountability.

2. **Leaders who exaggerate numbers have created for themselves their own personal obstacle of their leadership.** Dishonesty can not be a part of leadership. The very foundation of leadership is the integrity of the leader. When a leader feels compelled to misrepresent the situation through a numerical accountability the competitive spirit is an enemy of his/her soul.

3. **Leaders who exaggerate numbers are cutting themselves off from the blessing of God.** Jesus said, "Can a good tree bear bad fruit, can a bad tree bear good fruit?" Further, "Neither do people pick grapes from thorn bushes, or figs from thistles." And finally, "All bad trees will be cut down and thrown into the fire." (Matthew 7:17-20) Whenever numbers are involved we must remember that it is more than just a game—the honesty of reporting is a life and death struggle for the blessing of God on one's life!

The competitive spirit reaches much further than just numbers. This deceptive spirit can affect good leaders through the "image" they try to project to others. Cars, clothes, homes, and lifestyle are all things leaders sometimes use to manipulate what others think about them.

The first 4 verses of 1 Timothy chapter one begins with a greeting but quickly proceeds into a warning.

"Paul, an apostle of Christ Jesus by the command of God our Savior and of Christ Jesus our hope, to Timothy my true son in the faith. Grace, mercy, and peace from God the Father and Christ Jesus our Lord. As I urged you when I went into Macedonia, stay there in Ephesus so that you may command certain men not to teach false doctrines any longer, not to devote themselves to myths and endless genealogies. These promote controversies rather than God's work—which is by faith." (1 Timothy 1:1-4)

It is from this first section that the Apostle brings out three major problem areas of his day. These three problem areas give us insight into deeper dimensions of what this young church was going through.

11

The Apostle Paul frequently makes it clear that he wanted his life and work to mean something. We are able to witness just that attitude in how he relates to Timothy with regard to his place of leadership.

The Warnings:

1. **Don't give or initiate too much opinion.**

2. **Don't try to figure every thing out.**

3. **Don't resist.**

Don't give or initiate too much opinion. The warning from the Apostle neither is— "nor devotes themselves to myths."

Opposing opinions feed that negative competitive spirit. Opinions are really the culmination of thought processes. Some opinions are extremely strong, while others are weak. The difference between strong and weak opinions is the amount of intensity given to each opinion. The more intense, the stronger the opinion. The Apostle warns that we should rise above strong opinion. It is through Paul's vast experiences that he is able to see the stronger and longer one holds an opinion—the more closed one becomes to other's opinions and (to God). Strong opinions can and do become an obstacle that needs to be removed so a leader can be more effective.

ALWAYS TRY TO REMAIN "OPEN" NOT OPINIONATED!

Don't try too hard to figure it all out. The word study of "genealogies" has the meaning of "to trace back or to reckon." This concept of tracing back gives us the impression of trying to "figure it all out."

We waste too much time trying to figure it all out. The Apostle is showing Timothy that effective leaders must learn to accept things the way they are—not waste time on things about which you can't do anything.

Don't resist. Resistance usually results in our lives when questions and searching prevail. The best response to aggressiveness in controversy or excessive questioning is no response at all—don't resist.

It takes two people to argue—if one refuses (doesn't resist) there is no argument. My younger brother was an expert at this. Whenever we would begin to argue and then wrestle, my brother would go "limp" and end the confrontation. There was no longer anyone to fight against me.

Effective leadership chooses the fights to which to engage. A leader must choose its battles; at the very least the effective leader can choose to not react quickly to controversy.

One way to accomplish choosing your battles is to allow yourself three days before responding to criticism. Additionally, allow yourself one day before responding or reacting to things that push your emotional buttons.

A Great Attitude to Adapt for Effective Leadership is: "We are building a home here!"

If we look at verse 4 in chapter 1: "...rather than God's work which is by faith." The Apostle completes his initial warning with the positive attitude of building as an alternative to fables, genealogies, and questions.

The way to work through the potential dangers of competition is to view yourself as a house builder—building your spiritual house.

The house you are building is **your** house. There is no other house like it—and—there never will be. It is a house that is built where there is no room for a competitive spirit. Because one's spiritual house is so personal, it can't be compared to anyone else—which allows the competitive spirit to be removed.

The obstacle of competition isn't just about the Apostle's warning. The competitive spirit can be controlled in our lives. As you apply the following three principles, the competitive spirit will not be an obstacle to effective leadership.

14

PRINCIPLE #1: MOTIVATE PEOPLE -- DON'T MANIPULATE THEM.

Sometimes manipulation is not easy to recognize. It is always present when a leader works around, rather than through, a person.

Manipulation is easier on the leader to employ than motivation, which is why the leader should always choose to be the consummate teacher. Don't hurry through the instructions. Instead of poor communication and manipulation, take the time to teach and motivate.

When ever leaders have to lie or mislead, motivation has not occurred. Motivation is always real, honest, and clear. It doesn't take extensive training for a leader to become a motivator, only patience toward others.

PRINICPLE #2: LEAD PEOPLE--DON'T LEASH THEM.

To be an effective leader, bring people along with you. Build their trust and confidence first. People move from what they know toward what they don't know. Don't force them out of this pattern or you will be greatly disappointed (in them and in yourself).

Come along side people as they grow. Don't expect them to be animals on a leash that you teach tricks.

Take the time to personally build your leadership. There will be some people who will never trust you or follow your leadership. Don't take it personally when this happens. People will project their own weakness on to you. Learn to apply the

15

leading, not leashing principle; otherwise you will end up becoming resentful of those very people who can help you in becoming an effective leader.

PRINCIPLE #3: CHALLENGE--DON'T CONDEMN.

There is a huge difference between challenging and condemning. The problem is if people feel they are being condemned, they won't be able to accept the leader's challenge.

The best way to apply this principle of challenging is to set the tone by challenging yourself first. Step up and try for the best in yourself. Continue to grow and develop. Don't be afraid for others to see you sweat.

When people see this growth in you, they will be challenged themselves. Help them to develop and set goals. Guide them with high and clear expectations. When they see you trying and attempting to be real in your personal growth, they will work hard to accept any challenge that comes their way.

There are many dangers with the competitive spirit.

"The goal of this command is love which comes from a pure heart and a good conscience and a sincere faith. Some have wandered away from these and turned to meaningless talk. They want to be teachers of the law, but they do not know what they are talking about or what they confidently affirm. We know that the law is good if a man uses it

16

properly. We also know that the law is made not for good men, but for lawbreakers and rebels, the ungodly and sinful, the unholy and irreligious; for those who kill their fathers or mothers, for murderers, for adulterers and perverts, for s lave t raders, a nd l iars, a nd p erjurers—and for whatever else is contrary to the sound doctrine that conforms to the glorious gospel of the blessed God, which he entrusted to me." (1 Timothy 1:5-11)

The Apostle intensely relates the great price to pay if the competitive spirit is allowed to be present in leadership.

1. **Rebellion.** Rebellion is an enemy of effective leadership. It comes as justification and quietly seduces the mind into self-destruction.

2. **Irreligious.** This could b e described as "irreverent." Reverence is the key to peace in life. The competitive spirit does not stop until there is no peace, no reverence, and no rest.

3. **Murderers.** Those who are controlled by the competitive spirit eventually have no regard for human life, no matter whose life it is.

4. **Adulterers.** Leaders who are consumed in competition are not able to see moral issues clearly. As the morality line blurs, leaders can easily get caught in the web of moral sin.

5. **Perverts.** Perversion is no respecter of persons. It consumes one without an ability to recognize it has even become near. Perversion is a terrible thing, but gives us the picture of what can come through the door of the competitive spirit.

6. Liars. Dishonesty is a great danger, especially because it can be clothed and disguised—and above all—easily justified.

These dangers of the competitive spirit don't happen over night. These dangers develop gradually and subtly. Deeply seated in the obstacle of effective leadership of the competitive spirit—rebellion, irreverence, murdered, adulterers, perversion and dishonesty, make the words of a leader worthless and their leadership ineffective.

We don't have to be possessed by the competitive spirit. We can have ambition and drive. We don't have to allow the competitive spirit to be in control. We can be challenged and grow without having to be in control of everything.

There are **three qualities of success** that can help a leader be effective at many different levels. These are not often regarded as leadership material but without them in place a leader will constantly battle the obstacle of the competitive spirit. They help a leader be self-accountable and accountable to those he/she serves.

Qualities of Success:
1. A Pure Heart
2. A Clear Conscience
3. A Sincere Faith

QUALITIES OF SUCCESS: A Pure Heart.

The "heart" represents the core of the person—the thoughts, feelings and emotion. A leader who wants to be successful has to remain clean in thought, feeling and emotion. The only way to retain a pure heart is to make it a daily project.

- **Cleanliness of heart is insured through cleanness of thought.**

- **A clean thought life includes thinking the best of others—thinking the best of situations—thinking the best of things in general.**

- **Your mental focus sets the pace for the whole of your life. Keep yourself accountable for a positive mental focus.**

QUALITIES OF SUCCESS: A Clear Conscience.

We usually think of conscience as something that affects us "after the fact." The concept of the conscience used in the Bible was considered to be something done **beforehand**—"to see completely all the moral implications." This kind of perspective creates the opportunity for leadership to grow, mature and become more effective.

- **Each leader needs to completely examine moral issues within themselves.**

- **Leaders should be practical, yet firm, in their personal moral convictions.**

- What was once wrong—is still wrong—what is right will always be the truth.

- Every leader must be able to face each day they live with a clear conscience. Before making any decision, a leader must deal with the question of his/her own conscience first. How will you feel about this (about yourself) tomorrow?

QUALITIES OF SUCCESS: A Sincere Faith.

This idea of "sincere faith" means truthfulness. Truthfulness is essential in effective leadership. People need to be able to count on what their leader says. But it goes beyond that—truthfulness is based upon a person's life.

- A leader needs to be "real" if he/she intends to be effective.

- Don't be afraid of letting others see you sweat. It makes you a real person.

- Always remember that an effective leader is first a truthful and honest follower. There are no short cuts to effective leadership.

CHANGE: Wiping out the competitive spirit!

Change is the key to wiping out the obstacle of the competitive spirit. The belief in change in general and in my life personally is a key to leadership development.

The last section of 1Timothy chapter one reminds us about change:

PEOPLE DO CHANGE:

"I thank Christ Jesus our Lord, who has given be strength, that he considered me faithful, appointing me to his service. Even though I was a blasphemer and a persecutor and a violent man, I was shown mercy because I acted in ignorance and unbelief. The grace of our Lord was poured out on me abundantly, along with the faith and love that are in Christ Jesus." 1 Timothy 1:12-14

Here is Paul's own strong and convincing testimony: PEOPLE DO CHANGE BECAUSE HE CHANGED. Paul lists those unbecoming characteristics in his own life to underscore the fact that people do change.

NOT ONLY DO PEOPLE CHANGE—ANYONE CAN CHANGE:

"Here is a trustworthy saying that deserves full acceptance: Christ Jesus came into the world to save sinners—of whom I am the worst. But for that very reason I was shown mercy so that in me, the worst of sinners, Christ Jesus might display his unlimited patience as an example for those who would believe on him and receive eternal life. Now to the King eternal, immortal, invisible, the only God, be honor and glory forever and ever. Amen." 1 Timothy 1:15-17

The foremost belief brought out here is: We must fully accept that Christ came into the world to save sinners. With this in mind—because of what Christ did—people can change.

We must fully accept that with mercy from God and the patience of Christ, any one of us can change. This does require submission to obtain the mercy and a daily attention to change to obtain the exercise of the patience of Christ.

Change is always possible but there is a requirement—each person must want to change and fully accept that change requires constant attention to the relationship we have with God through Christ.

PEOPLE MUST BE PROMPTED TO CHANGE:

"Timothy, my son, I give you this instruction in keeping with the prophecies once made about you, so that by following them you may fight the good fight, holding on to faith and a good conscience. Some have rejected these and so have shipwrecked their faith. Among them are Hymenaenus and Alexander, whom I have handed over to Satan to be taught not to blaspheme." 1 Timothy 1:18-20

There are 3 things leaders do to help prompt people to change:

    1. Fight the good fight.
    2. Keep a good conscience.
    3. Hold onto faith.

The Apostle Paul depicts the rejection of change as a "shipwreck of faith." The competitive spirit is a "shipwreck of faith."

Leadership is like a ship. If a competitive spirit is allowed to become an obstacle through making everything only about doing better than someone else, the ship will wreck. The result is ineffective leadership wrought by isolated, lonely and selfish people. If a competitive spirit has become a part of your leadership style—repair your ship and send it back on the journey!

23

QUESTIONS FOR DISCUSSION

1. What are some ways the competitive spirit has affected your life personally? _____

   _____

   _____

   _____

   _____

2. Name and discuss some ways you have seen the competitive spirit affect the life of others or affected groups of people? _____

   _____

   _____

   _____

   _____

3. How could the three qualities of success listed in this chapter help you in your life? _____

   _____

   _____

   _____

   _____

   _____

4. What is the most difficult thing about change? ___

   _____

   _____

   _____

   _____

5. When have you seen someone change? Describe the circumstances and the result. _____

   _____

OBSTACLE #2
The Loss of Perspective

There is a children's game played in the snow called "Fox and Geese." It is started when all participants create narrow pathways through the snow by scooting their feet together. Once the pathway is all interconnected, the games begin. The rule is everyone must stay within the narrow path all the while moving as fast as they can. Because of the fast movement of the game and the number of people playing, the quick result is the total devastation of the pathways. The game is over because the boundaries are gone.

The same is true regarding effective leadership. We do fine for awhile but over the course of time through interaction, decisions, and communication we lose our concentration. The loss of concentration brings the loss of focus and hence, a loss of perspective concerning the work you are supposed to be doing. A loss of perspective is dreadful for those who are being led by a leader who has lost it. The leader is ineffective and either doesn't realize it—or does and has too much pride to do anything about it.

There are some "signs" to watch for that signal a person has lost their perspective:

DISINTEREST. The leader begins to show signs that the have "arrived." It will appear the leader is condescending or arrogant. The leader will begin to feel like people are stupid and aren't worthy of his/her investment of time. None of this is true (it is never true) but a leader who has lost his/her perspective doesn't realize it.

EXCUSES. Where once the leader used to be involved in certain things, now offers excuses to keep him/her from getting involved. The excuses are all logical and rational. Enthusiastic involvement gets replaced with excuses.

BLAME. One of the more acute signs of a loss of perspective is when the leader aims blame at others. When a leader uses blame to justify an area of responsibility, his/her leader is sure to be ineffective at most levels. Placing blame can be an indication of personal problems at a depth deeper than just the ability to lead others. No matter what the context is of an accusation, blame is never an acceptable venue for a leader. Leadership is, in its very nature, responsible.

UNFAITHFULNESS. When a leader has a change of lifestyle different than the one people once believed in (or signed on for) a spiritual problem has emerged out of a loss of perspective. The leader begins to have different priorities and spiritual things are not as important as before.

A LACK OF FRESHNESS. There is no substitute for a daily spiritual walk with God. A leader who has lost perspective is bored with spiritual things that once brought excitement. Where once there was spiritual freshness, now is only stale dryness.

THE WALK AND THE TALK DON'T MATCH UP. Things just don't add up. What the leader says and does are two different things. This is a leader who has lost perspective. This issue is potentially one of the most destructive because a leader who says one thing and does another is one who doesn't realize it is even happening. This person is usually unapproachable about the issue as well. People are very defensive about their behavior naturally—a leader who is saying one thing and doing another is a person who is clueless regarding his/her own behavior.

The Apostle Paul addresses his spiritual son, Timothy, in his letter regarding perspective. Knowing leadership is sometimes a lonely venture, Paul shows Timothy in chapter 2 how to keep, maintain, and recover perspective.

This study should help leaders at every level of their perspective. These men were experienced Christian leaders. Even though Timothy was young, he was seasoned. The instruction he is given transcends his situation—just like any of the Apostle Paul's writings it reaches across the centuries to help us with perspective even today!

Even though it is 2000 years old, Paul's writings reach across the centuries to help us with our perspective today!

KEEPING PERSPECTIVE

"I urge, then, first of all, that requests, prayers, intercession and thanksgiving be made for everyone—for kings and all those in authority, that we may live peaceful and quiet lives in all godliness and holiness. This is good, and pleases God our savior, who wants all men to be saved and to come to knowledge of the truth. For there is one God and one mediator between God and men, the man Christ Jesus, who gave himself as a ransom for all men. The testimony given

27

in its proper time. **And for this purpose I was appointed a herald and an apostle—I am telling the truth, I am not lying—and a t eacher o f the t rue faith t o the G entiles." 1 Timothy 2:1-7**

The first precept to explore is personal responsibilities in keeping perspective. These responsibilities are listed in verse one. These responsibilities apply to effective leaders' general outlook and priorities for life.

Requests. Requesting means to make our needs known. As a need arises, we let God know. We don't complain about our situation, we share it with God. The teaching of Jesus reveals that He knows what we have need of even before we ask—so the need to ask is for us—not for Him.

The same concept can be applied to the effectiveness of your leadership. Never expect people to be a mind reader. Make the need known. Don't be passive and expect others "to pick up on what you need." Don't expect them to "figure it out" or "get it." Your expectation should lie within yourself. Make your needs know clearly to those around you—not in a complaining tone—but in calm tones. **Make your request known to those who can help you!**

Prayers. Have you truly petitioned God with the concerns on your mind? Are you practicing a daily prayer life? The daily prayer life is the essential ingredient in keeping perspective.

This prayer time needs to include asking God if there are areas in which you need improvement. It is here that every leader should ask God to help them with keeping a proper perspective. Whenever a leader has lost perspective it can usually be traced back to when the daily personal prayer life began to dysfunction.

Intercession. The original Greek word indicates this word as an "interview." The idea of "interview" is important in considering my responsibility in reaching out to others. Praying for others helps in keeping perspective because it keeps one's eyes off self and on the needs of others. Intercession causes one to reach past one's self.

Thanksgiving. Every leader needs to be grateful. It needs to come both out of the words we speak as well as our actions and attitude.

A proper perspective can be most clearly seen in the grateful attitude of a leader. Thankfulness is the one of the first attributes to disappear when one is losing perspective.

The are some key "triggers" to our loss of perspective—watch out for them!

Watch out when you begin to have an attitude toward the authorities in your life! Authority, whether in the form of a person or the form of an organization, is easily noticed when a leader is losing perspective. Authority structures are targets because they are large in our lives.

When a leader begins to carry an attitude against authority, you will notice other attitude problems as well—it has been the attitude toward authority that triggered it. The Apostle Paul specifically mentions the idea of "kings" or in today's

29

understanding, this idea is the foundation of power. Overall, people tend to have a problem with power. Power persistently causes us to see things differently. Attitudes, about or toward authority or "power," corrupts our perspective.

Watch out when you begin to have an attitude toward people who do better than you! An effective leader must be able to quickly regain perspective if there is a tendency to be prone to be jealous toward those doing better than we are.

Learn to rejoice with those who win, do better, or score higher than you do. Usually we get "bested" by the same person time and again. Every leader needs to understand how it feels to be "bested" by someone else, so they know how it feels to those they lead. In general it is always for the best to realize there is someone always smarter, always faster, and always better than me. It is especially healthy for every leader to realize every leader answers to another leader. If you keep this perspective in the forefront of your mind, it will allow you the time to get your eyes off of others—and—on to growth!

The Apostle Paul teaches Timothy that a **peaceful life** is a result of keeping perspective. Peace, in the context he teaches it, means to "keep your seat" or "hold steady." It would only make sense that keeping one's perspective instills with the leader an ability hold steady and stay consistent in the long term. The peaceful life is a characteristic, as well as a blessing, that comes from keeping perspective.

Secondly, the Apostle Paul teaches Timothy that the **quiet or tranquil life** needs to be a characteristic of the leader. Unfortunately, tranquility of soul is absent in the life of many leaders. Instead of harnessing personal emotion and leading by removing the obstacles of effective leadership—many lead by their emotion. These leaders end up burned out, devastated, hurt, and often—destroyed. Keeping perspective helps to maintain accountability for the leader to manage his/her emotions and enhance the tranquil inner life.

Third, the Apostle Paul teaches Timothy about the concept of **Godliness**. Godliness is often misunderstood. It is one of the most powerful and purposeful words in the Bible. The Greek word for godliness, "eusebeia" means the entire gospel scheme—namely—the birth through a virgin; a sinless life; a crucifixion for sins; death; rising from the dead; ascension into Heaven—and **my involvement in the proclamation of this teaching**. Godliness takes life to a new level. It creates purpose for existence. It also takes an ordinary type leader and drives him/her with purpose of life at a new (and eternal) level. A leader who is (Godly) is driven with a passion for God and removes any obstacle of effective leadership!

Finally, the Apostle Paul teaches Timothy about **honesty**. This concept means more than just being truthful. Instead it means an open honesty that includes the "give and take" in relationships. A leader, who has lost perspective, is not able to be honest in relationships with those around him/her. A leader who has lost perspective spends most of his/her time trying to hide from people because of a fear of rejection.

Paul teaches Timothy that a leader can keep perspective through:
- **A peaceful life**
- **An inner tranquility**
- **Godliness**
- **Honesty in relationships**

31

MAINTAINING PERSPECTIVE

"I want men everywhere to lift up holy hands in prayer, without anger or disputing." 1 Timothy 2:8

This directive from Paul outlines a great experience of unlimited consecration with no restrictions for the leader seeking to maintain perspective in life and leadership.

"I want men..." means more than just the male species, but the entire human race—all the reasoning creatures that have ever lived.

"Everywhere" elaborates and fills in the gaps where the human race leaves off. It is an all inclusive term. There is no place to hide in all of life where one is unable to feel the power of God--the darkest jungles, highest mountains, deepest oceans, fartherest recesses of outer space—or— in the most stubborn, bullheaded leader!

"Everywhere" can also include those places we go to hide--the mental justification and logic we use to defend our behavior or attitude. God is **everywhere** and **fully aware**.

"Lift up...Rise up" can be applied to all the realms of our mental, emotional, spiritual, and physical existence. We are to rise up—way up—over those things that normally would bring us down. Leaders need to make it their life's work to learn to rise up rather than be brought down by their circumstances. There are so many potential things that can bring a person down—it is that rare person who decides (it is a decision of the will) that decides to take the high road and continue to look up.

32

"Holy Hands..." is a crucial step. The Biblical concept of hands is that of power. The idea of "holy hands" is the directive that the leader must surrender his/her power to God.

Have you ever been in a situation where you finally see that you are powerless to change a situation yourself? A leader finds this place from time to time. It is at the point of powerlessness that a leader is reminded of the necessity to surrender—surrender to God.

Leadership Exercise:

When you find yourself in a situation where you feel overwhelmed or "over your head":

Close your eyes and visualize turning the whole situation over to God.

"Prayer" is the word used for interview or intercession. It is not until you surrender your own energy to God are you ever effective in your prayer. You cannot be an effective leader if you fail to maintain your perspective; and you cannot maintain your perspective without constant and consistent prayer.

For what do we pray—or how do we pray? First, an effective leader surrenders him/herself over to God. Second, an effective leader describes to God the specific situations the leader is facing and asks God for the wisdom necessary to deal with them. Make notes and keep notes while you pray. The most effective leaders learn much about themselves and their situations while expressing things toward God in prayer. Keeping notes helps you remember what you learned during these daily prayer times. **An effective leader will see daily prayer as the most important meeting of the day!**

The Apostle Paul points out to Timothy there are emotionally charged issues that can prevent effective prayer from coming to pass. Specifically, Paul mentions—**anger and disputing**.

If anger is not managed it can cause a leader to be driven by emotion. If, as a leader, you don't manage your emotions, you can be sure your emotions will manage you. This is the emphasis the Apostle Paul is trying to make to Timothy and to all leaders.

Don't allow anger, lusts, or carnal passion to affect your life. Guard against these passions by concentrating on what you allow your mind to feed upon.

Disputing and conflict causes tension and frustration. When tension is present, one is not able to relax and feel the presence of God.

Resolve your conflicts quickly. Don't allow conflict to take your time or attention off the really important things on which a leader needs to focus.

> **Resolve any conflict quickly so that it doesn't interfere with surrendering your leadership to God.**

RECOVERING YOUR PERSPECTIVE

It appears the Apostle Paul has changed direction completely by addressing a problem of his day involving the leadership of women in Christian service.

When taken out of its context, this teaching regarding women and leadership can create resentment and division. Various interpretations and applications of this passage have caused pain and hurt feelings for years. The hurt isn't always obvious, but eventually it surfaces.

The best way to look at this scripture from I Timothy chapter 2 is in relationship to recovering your perspective. Women are used simply as an example for perspective. The illustration should not be taken personally or defensively. If it is taken offensively, the importance of the teaching will be lost.

We can't disregard what Paul is saying. This teaching is too important to removing the obstacles of effective leadership.

"I also want women to dress modestly, with decency and propriety, not with braided hair or gold or pearls or expensive clothes, but with good deeds appropriate for women who profess to worship God. A woman should learn in quietness and submission. I do not permit a woman to teach or to have authority over a man; she must be silent. For Adam was formed first, then Eve. And Adam was not the one deceived; it was the woman who was deceived and became a sinner. But the women will be kept safe through child birth, if they continue in faith, love and holiness with propriety." 1 Timothy 2:9-15

If you have ever lost your perspective the concepts found in this Biblical model will help you recover it. Every leader should use these as a check list for effectiveness.

Avoid drawing attention to yourself.

The Apostle Paul was dealing with real life issues. The men would not take the leadership role God intended, so women stepped into the void.

History bears out an important thing to keep in mind: The Apostle Paul used women at leadership levels all the time. He constantly named them in his Epistles and in other letters. He was always sincerely appreciative of their leadership.

Many would call Paul a chauvinist when putting men first. When doing so, the whole point of the teaching is missed. It is about **recovering your perspective,** not who comes first.

The Apostle Paul warns us regarding drawing attention to ourselves. Balance is the key to effective leadership. When we draw attention to ourselves we get our leadership out of balance, thus losing our perspective.

A leader's effectiveness is based upon the ability to maintain balance in:

- **Opinions**
- **Dress**
- **Communication**
- **Lifestyle**
- **Behavior—both public and private**

The illustration the Apostle Paul captures is "appropriate for women who profess to worship God." Instead of drawing attention to you, let your leadership lead people to God. Don't keep attention to yourself—turn it over to God. Do this deep with in your thinking and pass the concept on to others when put in the situation to do so.

Be a team player.

Examine how strong this sounds—**"A woman should learn in quietness and full submission. I do not permit a woman to teach or have authority over a man; she must be silent."** The Apostle Paul desperately wanted this young Church to develop a team player attitude. He wanted them to have the heart of a servant. He pinpointed an issue that he had observed in the Church.

Listen carefully to others.

We can't be listening to others if we are talking. We all talk too much. An effective leader listens more than talks. Learning to listen requires training yourself to do so. Listening opens up a whole new world of education and experience.

A good leader needs to be a good follower.

In every organization the leader is both a leader and a follower at the same time. Every leader answers and is accountable to another leader.

Every effective leader was first a faithful follower. This is true both internally and externally. It occurs internally in regard to the leader themselves—the leader needs to know what it feels like to be led before they lead. It occurs externally as the leader receives respect from others by knowing their leader was once in their position needing to be led.

You don't have to control everything.

The Apostle Paul deals with the idea of a leader feeling the need to dominate others. When people feel "controlled" by others they resent it and won't be led.

There is a natural course of things a leader learns to tap into. You don't have to fight every fight—and you certainly don't have to win every time. When a leader falls into the mentality that he/she has to fight, win and fight again, he/she will lose perspective. As a result, it will become an obstacle to leadership effectiveness.

Learn from your mistakes.

Experience is the best teacher because you have already paid the tuition! Learn from your own mistakes—and why not cash in? **LEARN FROM THE MISTAKES OF OTHERS AS WELL!** Every leader is provided naturally and in his/her environment everything necessary to be effective. The application of it is up to the person.

> **Learning from your own experiences is the best kind of education because you have already paid the tuition!**

There is a place for everyone—you don't have to "fix it."

God has a definite order. The Apostle Paul emphasized that He created man first then woman. God's natural order always surfaces if we don't interfere.

Leaders sometimes think they have to "fix" everything. When a leader becomes a "fixer" he/she miss the larger picture and the greater point. God is in control—an effective leader realizes he/she is God's instrument He uses—**but they are definitely not God.**

People have to find their own place. Some will respond well to their leaders—others won't. When a leader has subordinates who aren't responding properly remember to let people find their place. Many a leader has worn themselves out trying to get rid of someone only to find out later if they had left well enough alone the natural course of human interaction would have taken care of it.

A leader shouldn't be driven by what others feel about them. Emotions are fickle—especially the emotions of others. If it takes all our effort to manage our own emotions why do we think we can control the emotions of others through pleasing them?

Let people find their own place.

Get to know yourself.

If you know those areas you are weak—get people to help you in those areas. If you don't know your weaknesses, don't worry it is sure to surface shortly!

Once you know where you are strong use it to help others—don't use it against them.

Observe yourself—be honest—not too critical, but not too easy either. Learn and grow from your self-analysis.

The better you know yourself the more effective a leader you will be because you will not have to lose, and then regain, your perspective. A loss of perspective won't be an obstacle of effective leadership for you.

Lead like you are a parent—nurture and teach.

The Apostle Paul gives Timothy a lesson on the emotional aspects of life when talking about women and the performance of their maternal duties.

The Apostle says that this time of child rearing can be emotionally redemptive, as the woman allows it to create with in her a better person. Child rearing causes one to be humble because of all the things it reveals to a person about emotional weaknesses. This emotional redemption comes through the faithfulness of a mother in the areas of love, faith, and holiness. Allow child rearing to become a spiritual journey for one's soul.

This scenario of motherhood can be brought in and applied to effective leadership. One of the best ways to recover perspective is to think of leadership as that of a nurturing parent. Think of the possible applications in recovering your perspective:

- **A parent should not have to have the power struggle of "who is the parent anyway?"**

- **A parent does not have to force nurture and care— it happens naturally because of being a parent.**

- **A parent always puts the children first.**

- **There is a mutual love and acceptance.**

- **There are times of tension; rebellion; and conflict but that doesn't change the desire for everyone to be a family.**

It is a constant in life that people are comforted to know someone is in charge and that person cares about them personally. Effective leadership is able to keep that truth in perspective.

It always gives people comfort to know someone is in charge and that person cares about them personally.

QUESTIONS FOR DISCUSSION

1. When a leader blames others, what does that indicate? _____

_____

_____

_____

2. Have you ever known a leader whose "walk and talk" did not match? How did you respond to their leadership? _____

_____

_____

_____

3. Discuss the idea of "Godliness." How can you integrate it into your leadership? _____

_____

_____

_____

_____

4. How do you avoid drawing attention to yourself? What do you suggest to others? _____

_____

_____

_____

OBSTACLE #3
Ambition

Ambition is considered important in most organizations. It might even be a surprise to see ambition in a study of obstacles to remove to effective leadership. The truth is ambition is extremely self-centered.

If ambition is not harnessed successfully, it has the potential to be extremely dangerous and powerfully destructive.

On the other hand, if ambition is harnessed, it can become a powerful and effective tool of leadership.

The difference in how ambition is used is through the individual leader.

Selfish ambition is often neatly disguised; even to the point the leader doesn't realize their ambition level is dangerous. Every leader must take a personal assessment of his/her ambition level on a regular basis. A leader needs to stay on top of personal ambition through serious and honest self evaluation.

> **Ambition in itself is not an obstacle until it becomes selfish—then it is SELFISH AMBITION.**

Ambition in itself is not good or bad. There are different levels of ambition based upon energy level, drive, motive and attitude. Chapter 3 of 1 Timothy gives us some positive input concerning this potential obstacle of effective leadership.

First the Apostle Paul shows Timothy a proper kind of ambition. This "Biblical ambition" is in keeping with effective and positive leadership models. Next, the Apostle Paul outlines for Timothy the characteristics of those who supervise others effectively. Finally, the chapter concludes with a prescription for ambition. When applied properly, ambition can be an important asset for any leader to be effective.

BIBLICAL AMBITION

"Here is a trustworthy saying: If anyone sets his heart on being an overseer, he desires a noble task." 1 Timothy 3:1

The concept of ambition is found in the word **desire** which means **"to reach out after."** The Biblical idea for ambition is summed up in the sense of balance one applies when "reaching out after" something (anything).

The Apostle Paul emphasizes that ambition needs to be applied to leadership through our circumstances with exactness. Those who supervise others are especially responsible for a balance in regard to ambition.

Biblical ambition is defined as "reaching out after."

It is acceptable for any leader to "reach out after" greater areas of responsibility. The irony develops when we examine how this is actually applied in leadership today.

Leaders disguise their desire for greater ministry because they are afraid to be misinterpreted. It would be good if in the future there developed a greater openness on the part of leaders in what they were "reaching out after."

Many leaders need to develop relationships with other leaders on a deeper, richer level so trust will help honesty between each other to prevail.

Instead of openness many leaders (and potential leaders) hold tightly to what they are "reaching out after." The lack of trust between leaders creates a selfishness that corrupts the "reaching out after" into a selfish ambition that doesn't trust or need anyone.

> # Leaders should build relationships with one another—developing deep levels of trust.

BIBLICAL CHARACTERISTICS OF THOSE WHO SUPERVISE OTHERS IN LEADERSHIP

Even though it is found in the Bible, these important characteristics could be applied to effective leadership at any level.

Any supervisor has an awesome responsibility. The word for Bishop is (episkope) which means to "superintend."

"Now the overseer must be above reproach, the husband of but one wife, temperate, self-controlled, respectable, hospitable, able to teach, not given to much wine, not violent, but gentle, not quarrelsome, not a lover of money. He must manage his own family well and see that his children obey him with proper respect. If anyone does not know how to manage his own family, how can he take care of God's church? He must not be a recent convert, or he may become conceited and fall under the same judgment as the devil. He must also have a good reputation with outsiders, so that he will not fall into disgrace and into the devil's trap." 1 Timothy 3:2-7

The Apostle Paul creates a profile for supervision. This profile can be used both to examine potential supervisors and to develop the leadership of supervision.

This profile includes sixteen characteristics that develop effective leadership at many different levels. Each characteristic opens up the leader's personal and professional life.

46

The primary emphasis of supervision is placed upon character and character development. The professional habits of the supervisor seem to be of secondary interest to the Apostle Paul's profile. His only reference to the professional dynamic is the leader should not be a novice.

The 16 characteristics of a leader have to do with the personal life (character) rather than the professional habits of the leader.

Let's set out the sixteen characteristics of this leadership profile:

#1 Blameless. Don't contradict people openly. People don't respond well to leaders who are authorities on every subject. It actually illustrates insecurity when the leader thinks he/she has to come off like an expert. The leader must be gracious with others and not cut them off when people share opinions or point of views. Cutting people off will end up being the obstacle that cut off the lines of communication as well. When people feel they are being "cut off" they will be less likely to be open in other forms of communication. The leader who cuts people off is usually "clueless" that the communication has been cut off until something major happens that dredges up the problem. The only way to prevent this degenerative communication scenario is for a leader to occasionally analyze the level of communication he/she is having with those supervised. Honest appraisal is absolutely necessary at this level. If the leader realizes that communication is light, strained, or non-existent then something has happened that has caused those he/she supervises to feel put down or cut off.

#2 One Wife at a Time. The effective leader must firmly espouse monogamy. Many times moral issues are "unspoken rules" but the Apostle Paul believes things need to be made clear. If the leader is not married then the concept would be moral—if married, speaks to marriage. Either way the moral/marital behaviors are a reflection of character. The wife/husband of a leader ought to be the only object of the leader's earthly affection. No flirting between people is innocent flirting. Leaders must have standards and principles to live by in moral regard. Think through your moral standards before the situations come to you—a lack in this area is a character problem. Moral decisions are made with in the character of a person long before there is a temptation.

Marital vows are important at so many levels—and—important at so many different levels of leadership. If a leader has stood before God and repeated vows like: "For better or worse; richer or poorer; in sickness or in health; **forsaking all others as long as we both shall live,**" it is an indication of the leader's strength when observing these vows in his/her day to day lives.

A leader who is single must decide how to live a moral life as a single leader in the world. A married leader must decide how to live a faithful life in the world. Lust is out of place at any level when leading people.

Many leaders justify their lust by the "look but don't touch" attitude--that as long as you don't act upon what you are thinking--all is okay. **But that thinking is the problem!** Lust creates a life of fantasy that will rob a leader of any kind of effectiveness. Lust preoccupies your mind, robs you of your time, and becomes addictive.

Leaders who decide to guard their lives against lust of any form find success and a **clear conscious**. Leaders who push the boundaries of moral consciousness find themselves caught up in sexual addiction.

The Internet is of great advantage to any leader. The information age can provide leaders with information at their finger tips. It is a wonderful advantage in effectively leading and supervising people to have all the information necessary. There is a downside to the Internet to which every leader must be on guard. Around 95% of the websites on the Internet are pornographic. A leader, who gradually gets pulled in, finds a power that increases its grip. The amount of time and energy pornographic activity requires creates a leadership void in an organization.

The leadership dynamic in many organizations is often an amazingly hypocritical one—the very supervisors who fire employees because of internet and email misappropriations are ones who have lust/pornographic/sexual addictions themselves. Unless the leaders police themselves the productivity of the organizations they serve will suffer dramatically. Moral issues through Internet usage is an important obstacle to effective leadership that can not be ignored!

#3 Awareness. A person who leads effectively is aware what is going on around them. The person who leads/supervises others needs a sense of awareness of: current events; relationships; Biblical application; and personal needs/issues.

There is nothing "cute" about a "clueless" leader. When people who are supervised see in their leader a person who is not aware of their surroundings, productivity and creativity will diminish. Further, if this issue is not addressed in the organization as this occurs, it will experience a degeneration of morale and momentum.

A leader needs to stay up to date in their relationships with the next tier of leaders in their organization

---

How AWARE are you?

- **What is the name of the person who works for you?**
- **Name three things you know about this person.**
- **What has this person been doing well?**
- **What does this person need to do to develop their own leadership?**

Awareness creates the ability to be objective and open with those you supervise. Effective leadership is intended to provide for the ability for a leader/supervisor to be having an impact on others.

#4 Self Control. An effective leader can control him/herself. The idea of self control encompasses all areas of life and behaviors. This character trait should be reflected in health, exercise, diet, work habits, dress, and communication and so on. A person who supervises others should not condemn the perceived lack of self-control in others because it often is a reflection of the lack of self control in the leader. No one is ever perfect—but a leader can choose to be self controlled. The work that it takes to be self controlled can be harnessed from the energy previously used to be judgmental of others. It is important for effective leadership that the leader "clean his/her own front porch" and not be needling people they supervise.

#5 Orderly. An orderly life is seen on a different level than that of being self controlled. Orderliness involves the journey of personal and professional discipline. The life of a leader must be an orderly (disciplined) one. An effective leader is one who is self-motivated and self-policing—not needing anyone to stay on top of them or keep them "accountable." Orderliness is contagious in a person's life—a person who is disciplined in one area is usually disciplined in every area of life because discipline is a cognitive action of attitude and behavior.

All a leader needs to do is examine one or two areas of his/her life, and it will reveal orderliness (or not).

#6 Hospitable. Hospitable literally means "a fondness for guests." An effective leader needs to genuinely like people. The reason for the need of leadership is because people exist and need direction.

The concept "hospitable" does not mean a leader has to be a socialite, the life of the party, or a huge entertainer. It does, however, mean the effective leader does not see people as an imposition.

51

> # An effective leader DOESN'T see people as an imposition.

#7 Always A Teacher. An effective leader possesses the gifts and graces necessary to be a teacher of people. Remember that teaching hasn't happened unless the students have learned. The effective leader must be able to communicate concepts and vision in such a way the students will learn.

How well the people in an organization do their jobs is a direct result of how well they have been taught. The effective leader accepts this concept and is always seeking ways to be a better teacher.

The most effective leaders are ones who are constantly trying to improve themselves as teachers. The educational process is the best way to improve your work force. People start from what they know and are moved to what they don't know (moving them from the known to the unknown model). When people are made to feel they are stupid—they will never learn anything. The most effective leader is first an effective teacher.

> # The most effective leader is first an effective teacher.

#8 Mentally Stable. This concept is taken from the Apostle Paul's "not g iven t o m uch w ine." W ine a nd d runkenness in this context are signs of mental instability. The effective leader who supervises people should not need crutches. He/She needs to be able to hold steady and not have to use controlled substances to make one able to deal with the elements of leadership.

Leaders who depend on "cocktail time" to brave their world are not going to be able to be an effective leader over the long term. The dependency on alcohol and other drugs creates an even greater dependency on alcohol and other drugs—and henceforth—mental unstableness.

#9 Not Quarrelsome. An effective leader should avoid being quarrelsome. Leaders lose effectiveness if they spend their time being argumentative with others. Not only does a quarrelsome leader turn people off so that they don't listen—communication between people becomes nearly impossible.

An argumentative leader is not very approachable for those whom they supervise—and will eventually create huge productivity problems because people are zapped emotionally. The emotional drain created from just "coming to work" affects the energy level in the work place. This whole scenario can be tracked back to a supervisor who is unapproachable and argumentative.

A quarrelsome/argumentative leader is also difficult for those in a lateral management level with the leader. Those who work with this kind of person are generally frustrated and exasperated by it.

This kind of leader is also a frustration to his/her own supervisor. The person in authority over a quarrelsome leader should deal with the problem as soon as possible by exposing it and challenging them to build relationships, rather than use up their energy arguing with people.

Deal with a quarrelsome leader as soon as possible – Challenge the troublesome leader to build relationships.

#10 No Greediness Allowed. No effective leader has as his/her main motive personal financial gain. There is no room in effective leadership for the "wheeler-dealer."

Those who are supervised should never fear they will be taken advantage of by the leader. The workers should not think their leader is becoming rich, famous, or even personally advantaged by the workers' innovations or labor, without that leader sharing equally with the workers. This is not to say that aggressive personality won't be aggressive financially—nor is it to say that effective leaders should not do well materially and financially. What this is saying is—**financial gain should not be the motive for effective leadership.**

Effective leadership should be its own reward—and financial gain should follow that **(and it will)!**

#11 Patience. An effective leader is committed for the long term. He/She sees things in a broad perspective and a larger picture. Things are not about what happens right now—this minute—but how things develop in an organization over the long term. An effective leader realizes that nothing lasts forever and all things change. Things come in cycles and lasts for a season. A leader is effective in their situation if they remember to be patient and train themselves to endure the cycles of life and (cycles of leadership).

#12 Peaceable. The effective leader is the peacemaker in every situation. Peace should follow a leader wherever he/she goes. It should be peace—not confusion—that people in an organization should experience. An effective leader will create peace where confusion once was present.

Bringing Peace to Any Situation:
1. **Agree on what everyone agrees on.**
2. **Refocus and retain the focus on what you agree on.**
3. **Clear the air and let the wounds heal.**
4. **Give every space.**
5. **Don't try to "fix it" or "control it"—let it naturally fix itself. (By doing the above 4 things).**

#13 Content--Not Covetous. An effective leader needs to do their work and not worry about what others have or are doing. If the mind wanders to what others have or what others do, unnecessary attitude problems are created. A leader can become exhausted trying to keep up with others, without realizing the life of those coveted others may be sending those people deeply into debt.

An effective leader realizes nothing is how it appears. Your life should not be a life based upon someone else. Your life should be lived based upon you. Contentment with how circumstances, finances, social standing, etc. are right now frees the leader to become effective, which may open up huge doors of opportunity later.

#14 A Well Managed Family. A leader's family life is a reflection of his/her management ability. The family life is extremely personal and intense, which clearly reflects who a person really is in how their family operates and interacts.

The Apostle Paul instructed Timothy to observe a prospective leader's family, as the family life shows what kind of potential a person has to lead an organization.

> # If you want to see how effective a leader will be—look at their family.

#15 Maturity. The literal concept of maturity means "newly planted." The Apostle Paul doesn't spell out any age requirements of leadership or how old you have to be to be an effective leader. Maturity (not based on age) is being able to weave common sense with wisdom and adequately communicate those insights for others to understand.

> **Mature leadership is the ability to weave common sense together with wisdom--and then communicate it effectively to those you supervise.**

#16 Well Thought of By Others--Respect the effective leader is respected by others within and outside of the organization her/she serves.

Respect is brought about through fairness with all people and honesty in relating to them. Fairness and honesty creates a sense of immediate relationship building and trust, even with new acquaintances, business contacts, and by reputation from those who have never met the leader.

THE CHARACTERISTICS OF THOSE WHO ASSIST THE SUPERVISOR

The word used by the Apostle Paul in his instruction to Timothy is "deacon" which literally means to "wait upon." Hence, the application of the position of deacon to most organizations would be those who assist the one who supervises—either as assistant or a secretary.

As a leader, use these characteristics from First Timothy as a check list when interviewing or finding people to assist in the leader's work.

"Deacons, likewise, are to be men worthy of respect, sincere, not indulging in too much wine, and not pursuing

dishonest gain. **They must keep hold of the deep truths of the faith with a clear conscience. They must first be tested, and then if there is nothing against them, let them serve as deacons. In the same way, their wives are to be women worthy of respect, not malicious talkers but temperate and trustworthy in everything. A deacon must be the husband of but one wife and must manage his children and his household well. Those who have served well gain an excellent standing and great assurance in their faith in Christ Jesus." 1 Timothy 3:8-13**

If leaders would use Paul's 7 characteristics of assistants to guide decision-making for developing their leadership tier, they would save themselves hours of rough times.

#1 Honesty. The assistant must be one who will tell it like it is—no more, no less. A trustworthy assistant must be honest with themselves and with others.

#2 Consistent. The assistant needs to be consistent in lifestyle, attitude and communication. A person who is assisting an effective leader is sincere in communication. A consistent person would never be caught saying one thing to one person and another thing to another person. Consistency in what speech, attitude, and action is a vital characteristic.

#3 Stable. The assistant to the leader should not need of "crutches" to deal with the stress of work. An assistant needs to be stable and steady, not given to excess, obsess or addictions.

#4 Not Greedy. An effective leader will not let people assist who are in it for personal financial gain. An assistant should be well compensated, affirmed, and rewarded, but that should not be the reason for the work. The work itself should be the reason for involvement. The Apostle Paul calls this the "deacon" for a reason—because the person has a "calling" to serve and assist. An effective leader will not use an assistant that is always about the material or the discussions about it, or the complaining concerning it. The pursuit of personal financial gain will waste a lot of time, attention, and energy.

#5 Pure Motives. The person who assists a leader should never be a manipulator. Motives must be pure. If motives are pure, operations will run smoothly—if not—something will continually surface as a problem.

#6 A Good Reputation. An effective leader will listen to how people speak of the person they are considering for a position. A good reputation includes observation of lifestyle, attitude and communication. An effective leader won't use someone who has lifestyle issues different from the leader's own, regardless of how productive they appear. Further, an effective leader will observe carefully both the attitude and communication of the person they are considering for a position of assistance. Both the attitude and personal communication reveal what the future would be like working together.

#7 A Well Managed Family. In modern interviews, an interviewer is limited legally by the questions that can be asked—but that doesn't mean a leader looking for an assistant can't make careful, insightful observations.

A person's family is an extension of his/her life and leadership. The way prospective applicants have helped their family is the way they will help you. Observe their children, if you can. How their children treat them is how you will be treated by your assistants treat you in your leadership.

Family life is in a constant state of change in our culture. The idea of the "blended" family creates a whole new dynamic. A person you are considering to assist you may be living in the same house with children they didn't raise. No matter the family situation, it is advisable to observe how the possible assistant approaches, talks with, and relates to people their household. This will give you a good indication of their interaction capabilities with people they know very well—which could include how they communicate with your employees.

IS IT FAIR TO JUDGE A PERSON BY THEIR SPOUSE?

Actually a spouse provides insightful clues of a person's character—both from a selection and a development standpoint. Of course it is not "politically correct" to judge a person by their spouse—but it is wise.

A marriage makes two people one person. Often one spouse reflects everything positive and the other everything negative. One spouse might carry one strong characteristic and the other carry a strong weakness in the same area—this happens to naturally balance out relationships.

It might be illegal to require a spouse to be interviewed, but an effective leader will know about the spouse before using an assistant at any degree of serious responsibility. Getting to know a spouse can be can be revealing and helpful in utilizing your assistants to help you effectively lead.

The Apostle Paul mentions the spouse in regard to the deacon, but not the overseer. Either way, the four characteristics found in the spouse are universal. These are the basic distinctives you should know about a spouse of someone you are considering as an assistant for your leadership:

- **Honest**—with self; with the spouse; and with others.
- **Not Negative**—does not speak badly or critically against others.
- **Self Controlled**—in action, attitude, lifestyle and in the words that come out of their mouth.
- **Trustworthy**—able to keep people's confidences. Not inclined to "scoop everyone on the latest thing." The spouse is loyal to their "other half."

The Apostle Paul instructed Timothy to "test the deacon." Many times we are in such need for help that we don't adequately test the people we want to use to assist us.

A 3 Fold Test Before Hiring

1. **Is this person a proven and loyal follower?**

2. **Do their walk and their talk match each other?**

3. **How does this person talk about others they have worked with? Work for? (What they say is what they will be saying about you)!**

GODLINESS AND AMBITION

The Apostle Paul completes his instructions to Timothy using a spiritual mantra for Timothy to follow. Many will argue that a leader does not have to be a Christian to be effective. **The bottom line is an *EFFECTIVE* leader will be a student of the teachings of Christ.**

The Apostle Paul gives effective leaders a great formula to live (and lead) by.

"Although I hope to come to you soon, I am writing you these instructions so that, if I am delayed, you will know how people ought to conduct themselves in God's household, which is the Church of the Living god, the pillar and foundation of the truth. Beyond all question, the mystery of godliness is great: He appeared in a body, was vindicated by the Spirit, was seen by angels, was preached among the nations, was believed on in the world, was taken up in glory." 1 Timothy 3:14-16

According to this instruction—a Christian ought to know how to conduct themselves. There are six parts to this model that deserve our deep reflection.

"MANIFEST IN THE FLESH"

Manifest (phaneroo in the Greek text) means to "render apparent." Flesh (sarx) means the "external." Jesus constantly reminded his followers that when they had seen him they had seen the Father and vice-versa. God wanted to make a clear cut presentation of what He was, what He wanted us to know, what He expected of us, how we should live, and how we should think. He did all of this through the life of Jesus Christ on this earth.

When God puts something in motion, He does it through His creative being—His creative genius. The creative process is more than just a one time experience. It is an on going process. Christianity isn't just a one time experience—it is a moment by moment process of life.

God manifest Himself to us in the flesh. He has made it possible to manifest Himself to the world every day as believers allow Him to become apparent in their lives consistently. This is another example of the creative genius of God.

"JUSTIFIED IN THE SPIRIT"

Justified means to "render innocent"—in this case the innocence of the soul. Because God made Himself manifest in Christ, we can—by following Christ—be restored spiritually to innocence.

Although God was made manifest in the flesh, sin was also made manifest in the flesh. Although sin can be wiped out of the soul—it can't be wiped out of the flesh—hence, the body gets sick and dies (mortality). The body must face mortality—it must suffer pain and eventually die. It cannot be rendered innocent. The body is mortal. The justified soul is immortal, rendered thoroughly innocent.

"SEEN OF ANGELS"

Speaking in eternal terms—the redemption of the soul was something never seen before in all dimensions of the creative worlds. It is so mysterious that God's other creatures—the angels—were amazed at what God had done. Humankind is unique and very special. Humans have been given the ability to change their lives. Redemption should be celebrated, not taken for granted. The redemptive purpose in the human race has an incredible, eternal future as the redeemed remain faithful and obedient. The angels themselves sense something amazingly special occurring.

"PREACHED TO THE GENTILES"

Preached (kerusso) means "to speak boldly divine truth." Preaching is an important part of the **most** important message in presenting the divine truth.

Preaching has lost some of its respectability. It has sometimes lost the purpose of delivering the divine truth.

Instead of respectability, preaching is seen as a joke today. "Long, boring sermons" is how people view this aspect of personal development.

What does preaching have to do with the effective leader? **The effective leader will enjoy the preaching of the divine truth as an indication of his/her need for a higher power/higher purpose in their life.**

The idea of "Gentiles" in the phrase "preached to Gentiles" has a broad application. The inference means the preaching of divine truth has no limits. It should reach into people at all levels and situations.

"BELIEVED ON IN THE WORLD"

We need to have faith in God's orderly arrangement. This demonstrates the submission to the events in life as part of God's master plan.

There are times when we ask the "why" question. Our view of the circumstances is never as God-centered as they need to be. It is at these points of doubt and despair that we must surrender to God's order. All circumstances and situations in life must encompass faith into God's orderly arrangement. If we don't do this—we can't effectively lead others.

Many times in life faith in God's orderly arrangement will require all the hope and strength you can muster. The realization that there is a master plan is a great encouragement for all those who lead others.

"RECEIVED UP INTO GLORY"

Most leaders get so caught up in their role as leader that they forget there is always a bigger picture at work in their lives.

No matter who you are or how great your responsibility there is an existence past this one that is more expansive by far than our present reality. It is for this next reality we are working for today. No realization or meditation will cause a leader to raise the bar higher than simply realizing the things I do, the decisions I make, the lives I touch today matters—and even for all of eternity.

The most effective leader can keep ambition in check by realizing the greatest accomplishments in this reality pales in comparison to what can happen in the eternal realm.

This present existence could even be viewed as a "proving ground" of sorts. We work selfish ambition (and the other obstacles to effective leadership) out of our system so that we are ready for what God has in store for eternity!

AN EFFECTIVE LEADER THINKS IN TERMS OF ETERNITY OFTEN:

1. I am learning things today that will prepare me for eternity.

2. Thinking about an eternal existence helps me raise the bar in this temporal existence.

3. Realizing there is an eternal life, a higher power, and a greater purpose for me—takes my mind off my stress.

QUESTIONS FOR DISCUSSION

1. When have you ever seen ambition become dangerous? _____

_____

_____

_____

_____

2. The characteristics of an effective leader have to the inner life. How important is the character of a leader? _____

_____

_____

_____

3. Of the 16 characteristics of an effective leader (A) which ones would you say are part of your life? (B) Which ones would you say you need to work on a little more? _____

_____

_____

_____

_____

_____

_____

4. Describe a plan for yourself that would involve using the 16 characteristics of an effective leader as a tool to help you develop in your leadership.

_____

_____

_____

_____

OBSTACLE #4
Lack of Personal Perseverance

The fourth obstacle to effective leadership is the very core of personal and professional development—perseverance. If you can't stick with something, you will never get the full benefit of it. If you are not able to persevere, you won't become a strong leader.

Perseverance is first and foremost a character issue. The battle for personal perseverance happens deep inside the inner life and projects itself out from there.

The ability to persevere is the difference in any endeavor to success; to follow through; and to deeper understanding of yourself and others.

The idea that perseverance is beneficial comes from those who have done it and testify to the depth it has given them in all areas of their lives. Further, a leader will only be as effective as his/her ability to persevere through all the facets of leadership.

The Apostle Paul addresses personal perseverance in three ways with his teaching to Timothy. In Chapter 4 of 1 Timothy—Paul deals with persevering through controlling the influences in our lives. The second section deals with personal perseverance in the midst of a perverted world. Finally, Paul sums up the boundaries for perseverance by applying four important principles to the life of the effective leader.

"The Spirit clearly says that in the later times some will abandon the faith and follow deceiving spirits and things taught by demons. Such teachings come through hypocritical liars, whose consciences have been seared as with a hot iron. They forbid people to marry and order them to abstain from certain foods which God created to be received with thanksgiving by those who believe and who know the truth. For everything God created is good, and nothing is to be rejected if it is received with thanksgiving, because it is consecrated by the word of God and prayer." 1 Timothy 4:1-5

"Abandon the Faith"

The crucial point in persevering is introduced at the very beginning of this teaching. The original Greek word for "abandon" is (aphistemi) which means to instigate a revolt—a revolt of one's faith.

It always comes back to the fact that the most effective leaders have a dynamic and personal faith in God.

The breakdown in leadership will come first in the breakdown or degeneration of personal faith:

- When the things a leader once held as absolutes of truth become clouded by the circumstances of life.
- When spiritual convictions become neutralized through the influences of others.

- When the leader begins to be pulled into activities that he/she knows to avoid but finds it to be a personal "outlet". This outlet becomes a preoccupation—then an addiction.

There are other things that create an environment for a leader to "abandon the faith"—stress, crisis, tragedy, loss or devastation all create the possibility to be hurt spiritually. But generally, it is not the huge thing that causes the inner life of an effective leader to lose out. It is through inconsistency, lukewarm conviction, or straddling the fence on personal issues instead of being resolute that causes one to "abandon the faith."

The basic problem is we receive so much information (input) that we have lost our ability to listen, process, and then make a decision as to our personal reaction. Instead we are inputted so much, so fast, that we don't have a chance to react. The inability to process and react creates an acceptance (as unintentional as it seems) to the input. It is this scenario the Apostle Paul refers to as "deceiving spirits." We are literally pulled in mentally by the input we receive because it is so much so fast. This is why so many people are down on the media. Whether television, the movies, or a newscast—we are receiving vast amounts of information without any ability to decipher, research, or process it.

Yet, a leader can still be effective despite the input they are receiving. The Apostle Paul illustrates it through two important phrases:

1. **The hypocritical liar**—the thing this leader says or teaches is believable and seems to be the truth. However, the leader is lying—but—there is no way to really tell they are lying. This is why perseverance is essential. The effective leader doesn't buy into everything he/she hears. Effective leaders listen,

process, and react to the input. One way an effective leader neutralizes the hypocritical liar is to see if their "walk and talk" matches up.

2. **The seared conscience**—the word "seared" means "rendered insensitive." There are few things worse than a person or group who has an insensitive conscience. They teach or speak extremely dangerous input to the life of the effective leader. The Apostle Paul uses two teachings as examples of the types of things a leader will hear and have to decide the validity through out—one was a teaching of his day to forbid people to marry—and another was to abstain from certain foods.

The deadly dimension to the fast paced input and the inability for us to process it is--**it weakens us.** Our energies get misplaced and we become weak internally.

However, there is something we can do to prevent the input we receive from hurting us deeply. Through an adjustment of attitude, we can be ready for any kind of input.

The Proper Attitude for Personal Perseverance:

The first attitude we must maintain is everything created by God is good. Perseverance weakens when we start to see things negatively or chaotically. Everything God created is good. We can see life as good and enjoy our lives.

The second attitude we must maintain is to show respect to all of God's creation. God's creation is all encompassing. We are not to judge any of his creation—that is God's job.

The third attitude we must maintain—especially when processing input—is to receive everything with thankfulness. The thankful spirit is the greatest asset one can have to personally persevere in the midst of the negative input. Thankfulness is a defense, but is also a powerful offensive tool to help increase the effectiveness in the life of the leader. A person who is genuinely thankful is a magnet for others to follow.

The fourth attitude we must maintain is to take the time to be spiritually awakened every day. "Prayer" is just a thought if we never do it—or a guilt trip that we go on if challenged with it. But prayer is only one dimension of a leader's spiritual life. A leader needs to take the time to set the pace of the spiritual part of his/her inner life every day.

PERSEVERANCE IN THE MIDST OF A PERVERTED WORLD

"If you point these things out to the brothers, you will be a good minister of Christ Jesus, brought up in the truths of the faith and of the good teaching that you have followed. Have nothing to do with godless myths and old wives tales; rather, train yourselves to be godly. For physical training is of some value, but godliness has value for all things, holding promise for both the present life and the life to come. This is a trustworthy saying that deserves full acceptance (and for this we labor and strive), that we have put our hope in the living God, who is the Savior of all men, and especially of those who believe." 1 Timothy 4:6-10

Sometimes you have to just hold on. Holding on is what perseverance is actually all about. Many people start out pretty strong, and then begin to falter.

Whether it is those tragic and traumatic circumstances or just the day to day struggles, effective leaders can be chiseled down to where they have lost their effectiveness. The Apostle Paul gives Timothy five things in his instructions that help to keep "holding on."

(1) Allow Illumination—"Point out things to the brothers." 4:16

We must be open enough to allow weaknesses to be pointed out to us—so we can be helped. Illumination is like turning on a light in a dark room. It happens quickly, so watch your eyes. Often the darkness has been present so long; it will take a minute to get used to the brightness.

Defensiveness will prevent illumination from having its full impact. Defensiveness originates from a feeling of insecurity. It can make hearing ears turn deaf to a suggestion. Stay open and teachable and you will always find illumination something that will help to succeed in perseverance.

Not all things pointed out by others are of benefit. It is, however, important that the leader listens. If a leader has a hard time taking suggestions, then illumination will be nearly impossible.

> **Train yourself to at least be able to take in all suggestions—you don't have to apply everything, but people need to feel like they have been heard.**

The other part of this is we need to help illuminate others. The ones who like to point things out to others are usually the ones least qualified to do so. Anyone who is honest and sincere knows that pointing things out to others is grueling work.

When should you or should not you point something out? The answer is as basic as another rule (but there is also another question). When should you tell someone about something on their clothes they can't see? The answer: **When they can do something about it.** You don't point something out if they can't do something about it—only when they can.

(2) Grow up—"Brought up in the truths of the faith."

Grow up in the faith! Have you grown any this week? If you don't grow, you will shrivel up.

Growth means to continually learn. The education of life comes all day long at every level. An effective leader is constantly learning and growing because he/she is always open and teachable.

Those activities we procrastinate and want to avoid are actually the circumstances that will teach us the most. Additionally, the people we would like to avoid teach us the most about ourselves.

Perseverance is impossible if we are trying to hold our breath and push ahead—but it becomes possible if we decide we are going to seize every opportunity available to us to grow.

(3) Avoid tangents—"Having nothing to do with godless myths and old wives tales."

Tangents are energy zappers. They drain a leader's ability to hold on.

A leader can be drawn into a tangent through logic, sincerity, or even one's own belief system. Whatever the reason—a person prone to a tangent wastes time, productivity and creativity.

One of the signs of a leader given to tangents is that they are emotionally up one minute and down the next—he/she gets suddenly excited and then depressed.

(4) Go into training—"For physical training is of some value, but godliness has value for all things, holding promise for both the present life and the life to come." 4:8

The vision of the effective leader for their own leadership needs to be "I am in constant training for the big race. I am getting into the best shape of my life. I am developing my abilities and skills to be of greater effectiveness and influence. My impact is being broadened through my training. I am in training so I will be ready for whatever the future holds for me."

Training is a life long endeavor. Personal perseverance comes along with the vision of seeing training for the long haul, always anticipating the next opportunity.

(5) Put your full hope in God—"We have put our hope in the living God, who is the Savior of all men." 4:10

Personal perseverance comes not from placing your confidence in the t emporal t hings of life, but into eternal principles and values.

A leader's confidence level has to come from a higher power or else it will vacillate along with emotional surges. God is the same—He does not waver. If a leader develops his/her confidence in a faith of a higher power/eternal being then one's sense of confidence will become an eternal destiny. This will shape one's sense of purpose and value on this planet.

BOUNDARIES FOR PERSONAL PERSEVERANCE

A boundary is a tool of communication. Looking from the outside, a boundary will communicate the limits. Looking from the inside, the boundary communicates the potential.

Fences are used in land boundaries to keep things in—or— to keep things out!

Like any fence boundary the boundaries for personal perseverance has four sides. Personal perseverance can grow or weaken. As the four boundaries are enforced they help to strengthen personal perseverance.

76

"Command and teach these things. Don't let anyone look down on you because you are young, but set an example for the believers in speech, in life, in love, in faith, and in purity. Until I come devote yourself to the public reading of Scripture, to preaching, and to teaching. Do not neglect your gift, which was given to you through a prophetic message when the body of elders laid their hands on you. Be diligent in these matters; give yourself wholly to them, so that everyone may see your progress. Watch your life and doctrine closely. Persevere in them, because if you do you will save both yourself and your hearers." 1 Timothy 4: 11-16

Boundary #1—SET AN EXAMPLE

The concept of "example for believer" is similar to the idea of "leading by example." Be a leader in everything you do and you will become an effective leader in everything you do.

Don't do things yourself that you wouldn't want others to do—especially those you supervise.

The Apostle Paul listed five areas where a leader should be an example:

1. **Speech—set an example in the things you say.**

2. **Life—let your behavior be the example.**

3. **Love—benevolence should be theme of your life.**

4. **Faith—set firm personal convictions, values, and principles of life and live firmly by them.**

5. **Cleanliness—clean thoughts; clean talk, and clean in personal hygiene.**

The idea of leading by example should be something that naturally comes along with leadership. Leading by example does not have to be a heavy or cumbersome burden.

Sincerity and purity can go hand in hand if a leader desires to be effective in the task of leading.

Boundary #2—DEVOTE YOURSELF

"Devote yourself" literally means to concentrate on something. Concentration needs to be strong in order to persevere. If concentration weakens, so will perseverance.

The Apostle Paul lists for Timothy three things Timothy could do in order to maintain his concentration for personal perseverance. Although specific to Timothy, the application is timeless (and general).

1. **Read the Scripture.**

2. **Encourage people on an individual basis.**

3. **Always be a teacher, providing people with instruction, and training them to be purposeful in their endeavors.**

Concentrating on these three directives will help strengthen the effective leader to persevere naturally through all the situations he/she faces in leadership.

Boundary #3—DON'T BE DISTRACTED

Distractions are common place today. Leaders are constantly tempted to lose their focus and become distracted by the mundane and minuscule. "Don't neglect your gift" is Paul's instruction to Timothy.

Focus on your leadership—don't become focused on whether colleagues or coworkers like you or not—lead them.

Boundary #4—BE DILIGENT!

Keep a good look out! Don't get tripped up. There are two areas to be vigilant:

1. **Watch your life**—Don't get pulled into a pattern of behavior that is not yours. Continue to develop into the sincere person you started out to be. If there is ever a time you realize something has personally changed— stop and start over again. Don't allow yourself to ever be something you are not.

2. **Watch your values**—Keep a close eye on what you believe, how you live it out, and what you are saying to others. Walk your own talk.

Personal perseverance goes a long way in leadership. It speaks volumes in unspoken ways to the people you are leading. Many leaders give up and quit because they have not developed boundaries of personal perseverance into their lives. Some leaders believe in a "do as I say not as I do" mentality. These leaders burn out quickly.

Effective leadership is not a short term ideal. It is a long term, persevering model that comes as the leader sincerely lives a life of strong principles and values, learns throughout life, and encourages those he/she leads.

QUESTIONS FOR DISCUSSION

1. Do you ever think of just giving up and quitting? Specifically, what brings on this feeling? _____

   _____

   _____

   _____

   _____

2. What do you need to set in place to help you process the input you receive on a daily basis? _____

   _____

   _____

   _____

   _____

3. When did you recently notice someone's walk and talk did not match? When was the last time you noticed it in yourself? _____

   _____

   _____

4. What would it take for you to be more thankful on a daily basis? _____

   _____

5. How did you react the last time someone pointed something out to you about yourself? When w as the last time you pointed out something to someone else?

   _____

   _____

   _____

   _____

   _____

   _____

   _____

OBSTACLE #5—Leadership Dysfunction

It seems obvious that leadership dysfunction would be an obstacle to remove to effective leadership, but from the appearance, many organizations do not seem to mind dysfunction.

Why would leadership dysfunction be allowed to continue in an organization when dysfunction is known as common place?

- Maybe the organization is relieved to have leadership dysfunction as it challenges the "comfort zone."

- Maybe the organization truly doesn't know any better. They think it is "par for the course" to have dysfunction among the leadership tier.

- Maybe those directing the organization like having someone (or something) to blame for their own short comings.

- Maybe the organization doesn't realize that leadership dysfunction is an obstacle to effective leadership that **can be** removed.

In chapter five of First Timothy, the Apostle Paul has a great deal to say about leadership in general. There are many examples to wade through to make the broader application to leadership dimensions.

As we are able to make our way through this fifth chapter, personal leadership dysfunctions will quickly surface.

There are ten basic dimensions of leadership the Apostle Paul mentions. He leaves us the liberty to apply his direction. In a sense, the opportunity Paul provides through instruction and application is the most basic way to remove the obstacle of dysfunction in leadership.

Dimensions of Leadership
1. **Style 5:1-2**
2. **Direction v. 3-8**
3. **Judgment Criteria v. 9-10**
4. **Asserting v. 11-15**
5. **Discernment v. 16**
6. **Compensation v. 17-20**
7. **Impartiality v. 21**
8. **Cautions v. 22**
9. **Stress v. 23**
10. **Dynamics v. 24-25**

These ten leadership dimensions have an array of applications. Each of them serves the purpose to remove the obstacle of leadership dysfunction so that leadership is effective!

1 -LEADERSHIP STYLE

"Do not rebuke an older man, but exhort him as if he were your father. Treat younger men as brothers, older women as mothers, and younger women as sisters, with absolute purity." 1 Timothy 5:1-2

There is one leadership style that is the most acceptable in all applications—"the family attitude." It involves treating those you supervise with the love and affection you would treat beloved family members.

The family attitude idea of leadership is meant to mirror a family which loves and respects each other—not a bitter, disrespectful situation. The Apostle Paul was assuming of our era was the same as his—they loved and respected one another.

The parent-child relationship is the most basic of life. It is therefore appropriate to observe this concept in relating to others. As a leader, treat people younger than you the way you would want someone to treat your child when you are not around to protect or defend. Also, treat those older than you the way you would want others to treat your parents if you were not around.

When a leader has to chastise someone older who is under his/her supervision, the respect shown should be that of a parent/child. In the Hebrew culture, the son greatly revered the father.

The "thought" life o f a leader also n eeds to c ome u nder this same rule of respect. People of the opposite sex should be thought of as brothers and sisters, not sexual objects. The leader should always have a clean, pure mind when dealing with others of the opposite sex.

2 - LEADERSHIP DIRECTION

"Give proper recognition to those widows who are really in need. But if a widow has children or grandchildren, these should learn first of all to put their religion into practice by caring for their own family and so repaying their parents and grandparents, for this is pleasing to God. The widow who is really in need and left all alone puts her hope in God and c ontinues n ight a nd d ay to p ray a nd t o a sk G od for help. But the widow who lives for pleasure is dead even

while she lives. **Give the people these instructions, too; so that no one may be open to blame.** If anyone does not provide for his relatives, and especially for his immediate family, he has denied the faith and is worse than an unbeliever." 1 Timothy 5:3-8

- **The effective leader's direction is to treat those in need as if they were a priceless treasure.**

The purpose of leadership is to meet the needs of people—not for pride, power, position or ego. The leader must make his/her trend toward people, not away from them. People are the reason for leadership. If there weren't any people, there wouldn't be any leadership. Leadership dysfunction always has a measure of dislike and disinterest of people. The purposeful direction of effective leadership is to meet the needs of people.

- **The effective leader's direction is to accept responsibility and train others to accept responsibility.**

The Apostle Paul uses widows with surviving family members as an example that each family must accept responsibility to help their own. The same is true of every single organization that exists. One of the major causes of leadership dysfunction is when people feel isolated and alone—they feel like they are carrying everything themselves. Valid or not, the emotional toll it takes on the leader and the organization who feels isolated sets the tone for leadership dysfunction. The only meaningful way to dispel this isolating dysfunction is through the acceptance of the responsibilities.

- **The effective leader's direction is to depend on God and help others in that direction.**

People need to depend on God rather than to seek pleasure. We live in a pleasure-seeking society that affects every level of life. Organizations are not exempt from being controlled by pleasure seeking even in the work place.

Leadership falls into dysfunction when the leader begins to seek pleasure more than effective leadership. The organization will follow the leader in this regard. When the leader is a seeker of pleasure, the people in the organization will fall into the same pattern.

- **The effective leader's direction is to always teach.**

The suggestion the Apostle Paul uses here is "infidel" which literally means the "uninstructed." People need to be taught—but not as badly as the leader needs to teach. Effective leaders learn by doing. Leaders often must "fake it until they make it." Teaching requires a leader to give his/her full attention to the thing(s) being taught. The leader gets a double dose of the learning through the study **and** presentation of information— thereby preventing the development of dysfunctional leadership.

3 -LEADERSHIP JUDGMENT CRITERIA

"No widow may be put on the list of widows unless she is over s ixty, h as b een faithful to h er h usband, a nd i s well-known for h er good d eeds, s uch a s b ringing u p children, showing hospitality, washing the feet of the saints, helping

those in trouble and devoting herself to all kinds of good deeds." 1 Timothy 5:9-10

Using the Apostle's thoughts as a model, we can formulate some important judgment criteria for effective leadership.

First, we should help those who can't help themselves, not those who will not help themselves. The Apostle Paul uses the "over 60" idea as someone who can't help themselves. Today we can't put an age to it, but we can put a need level to it. Leaders run into this dilemma all the time in their leadership—who should you help? Who should you cut loose? Who just needs some space? Who will get over it?

Second, don't help people who are living immoral lives. The reason is—people who live immoral lives lack an amount of important character ethics that should be guiding their lives. When character does not drive their lives, who knows what is next? Who will they tell the next lie to? Because a person who is immoral will lie about it, too!

Who should an effective leader spend his/her time helping verses who is going to create leadership dysfunction?

Can you tell how selfish the person is? A selfish person is a time waster and energy zapper. An effective leader learns to replace a selfish person as soon as possible—or leader's personal leadership will fall into dysfunction.

Is the person open to others? Openness will give the leader an indication on how quickly the bottom line can be uncovered when difficulties surface. Difficulties are bound to emerge in any organization. If your people are "stand offish," "noncommittal," or "closed off," you won't be able to get to the bottom of things when problems arise.

Does the person you need to help ever help others in any situation? Have you ever seen this person help others? The answer to this question will tell the leader is he/she is wasting time and energy. A person who reaches out and helps others is worth reaching out and helping. A person who does not reach out a nd h elp o thers i s n ot w orth h elping b ecause that p erson will always want more.

4 -LEADERSHIP ASSERTIVENESS

"As for y ounger widows, d o n ot p ut t hem o n s uch a l ist. For when their sensual desires overcome their dedication to Christ, they want to marry. Thus they bring judgment on themselves because they have broken their first pledge. Besides, they get into the habit of being idle and going about from house to house. And not only do they become idlers, but also gossips and busybodies, saying things they ought n ot to. S o I c ounsel y ounger widows t o marry, t o have children to manage their homes and to give the enemy no opportunity for slander. Some have in fact already turned away to follow Satan." 1 Timothy 5: 11-15

Leaders often struggle over the best balance for assertiveness. There are definite "do's" and "don'ts" regarding the arena where an effective leader asserts him/herself in a given situation.

The scenario the Apostle Paul creates for the young widow has broad applications for leadership assertion. Most leaders face decision-making many times in a day. Often a leader is forced to make a decision without all the necessary information. Other times decisions are "ad-hoc" rather than carefully considered. Decision making doesn't always reflect on leadership as much as it does upon work pressures and intensity.

Mistakes will be made even by the most effective leaders. The only time mistakes are never made is when the leader is doing absolutely nothing—and therefore ineffective.

The only leader that never makes a mistake in decision making is the one never making a decision—and is therefore doing absolutely nothing!

There are three general principles to guide leaders when they should be assertive. These principles are not all-inclusive but it is important to realize assertion in effective leadership is guided by balanced principles. Strong, assertive leadership all the time creates tension and discontent. Leadership that never asserts is often ineffective.

- **Always be assertive when you notice someone is slipping during your "watch."**

- **Always be assertive when someone under your leadership is a malicious talker.**

89

- Always be assertive when a home is in trouble.

The balance in assertive leadership is—**don't sweat the small stuff and yet don't let things get so huge they are hard to deal with!**

5-LEADERSHIP DISCERNMENT

"If any woman who is a believer has widows in her family, she should help them and not let the church be burdened with them, so that the church can help those widows who are really in need." 1 Timothy 5:16

Every effective leader has a measure of discernment. Some discernment is developed from experience—some is natural—some is trained.

A leader should accept the fact that he/she will not always accurately discern a situation. However, every leader should make it his/her goal to assess and discern each situation (or person) on individual merits and not prejudice or presupposition.

6-LEADERSHIP COMPENSATION

"The elders who direct the affairs of the church well are worthy of double honor, especially those whose work is preaching and teaching. For scripture says, 'Do not muzzle the ox while it is treading out the grain,' and 'the worker deserves his wages.' Do not entertain an accusation against an elder unless it is brought by two or three witnesses. Thos who sin are to be rebuked publicly, so that the others may take warning." 1 Timothy 5:17-20

Compensation is one of the most sensitive issues on the face of the planet! Whenever you are dealing with compensation you are dealing with a person's worth to their organization—which—no matter how hard you try—can never be separated from a person's self worth.

Few subjects are more volatile than what a person gets paid. Nothing is more discussed than what the leader gets paid—because everyone in the organization relates and compares themselves to their leader.

The Apostle Paul presents the whole issue of leadership compensation in such a way there is no ignoring it. There are several concepts Paul emphasizes:

- **Discussions concerning compensation should not be avoided. They should be honest and open.**

- **Leaders are worthy of their compensation.**

- **How much a leader gets paid should be a reflection of how well they lead. How well they do is the bottom line.**

- **Those who do really well—should be compensated really well—even double what others make. Especially those who have the total responsibility of an organization (those who preach and teach in the Apostle Paul's example).**

Although not intended to be a side-note, it could appear to be so—the Apostle Paul touches on accusations brought against the one in leadership of an organization.

Organizations should take note of the importance to have guidelines in place when someone accuses a leader of something.

- **For any accusation to be recognized as valid—it must be validated by two or three eye witnesses to the offence who are willing to step up and say so.**

- **If there are complaints at any level against a leader it must also be validated by two or three people who are personally affected by the issue.**

- **If the accusations or complaints are validated, the leader should be dealt with in retribution to the offense—depending on the number of people affected by the offence.**

7-LEADERSHIP IMPARTIALITY

"I charge you, in the sight of God and Christ Jesus and the elect angels, to keep these instructions without partiality and to do nothing out of favoritism." 1 Timothy 5:21

An acute problem that creates a good deal of the leadership dysfunction that exists is that of partiality. The reason partiality is such a problem is most leaders don't even realize it when they aren't objective, show favoritism, or display prejudice.

An effective leader will always guard against prejudice of any form. P rejudice against a p erson's c olor, o rigins, e thnics, o r preferences should never affect a leader's perspective about someone they supervise, work with, or deal with personally or professionally.

An effective leader will start off each day fresh and new. Wiping the slate clean with regard to people does not mean to be stupid or ignore the obvious—but it does mean to allow people a fresh start every day to succeed without prejudice or stereotyping of any kind.

8-LEADERSHIP CAUTIONS

"Do not be hasty in the laying on of hands, and do not share in the sins of others. Keep yourself pure." 1 Timothy 5:22

This eighth dimension gives us three solid and sound cautions:

- **Don't commit yourself too quickly in supporting others. Check things out first.**

- **Don't just sit by letting unethical practices occur under your watch.**

- **Stay up to date. Always remain on good terms with others. Don't let things build up over time.**

9-LEADERSHIP STRESS

"Stop drinking only water, and use a little wine because of your stomach and your frequent illnesses." 1 Timothy 5:23

Because of their close relationship, the Apostle Paul knew Timothy on a personal level. Paul knew first hand that Timothy was often a "stressed out" young man. Paul was concerned about Timothy and prescribed wine as kind of a medication for Timothy. The Apostle Paul was no doctor, but knew that Timothy's stress could kill him.

Every leader needs to be aware of the danger of stress. Stress robs a leader of his/her health and vitality.

Diet and exercise is the best way to deal with the stresses of leadership. Every leader should take special care and caution in these areas. Every organization should encourage the leadership to manage their stress (and provide them with the opportunities to do so).

10-LEADERSHIP DYNAMICS

"The sins of some men are obvious, reaching the place of judgment ahead of them; the sins of others trail behind them. In the same way, good deeds are obvious, and even those that are not cannot be hidden." 1 Timothy 5:24-25

The main dynamic of effective leadership can be summed up in one phrase—**"everyone reaps what they sow."**

Our deeds follow us along—and become obvious through the result.

Hence, if an effective leader pursues good deeds—that will be the dynamic that will follow his/her leadership.

Pursuing good deeds, good things, and good ideas, all with a good attitude will remove the obstacle to effective leadership of leadership dysfunction.

QUESTIONS FOR DISCUSSION

1. Describe what a family attitude looks like in leadership. _____

_____

_____

_____

2. What are the best criteria to use when wondering whether to help someone? _____

_____

_____

_____

3. When should a leader be assertive?   How is assertiveness applied in leadership? _____

_____

_____

_____

_____

4. What are some leadership cautions? _____

_____

_____

_____

5. What is the most important concept to remember about leadership dynamics? _____

_____

_____

_____

_____

_____

OBSTACLE #6
Secular Concerns

The idea of "secular concerns" as it relates to a leader refers to those other concerns that would rob an effective leader of his/her ability to stay focused.

Concerns outside a leader's spiritual life, family life, and work life cause a person to become distracted. Secular interest can creep in and threaten a leader's effectiveness. The effort the leader would use to do something productive has been drained by the secular interest.

A leader cannot serve an interest in secular concern without in some way hurting his/her effectiveness in leadership.

A LEADER CAN'T SERVE A SECULAR INTEREST WITHOUT IT IN SOME WAY HURTING HIS/HER EFFECTIVENESS.

There is a balance that can be achieved if the leader sets and executes the right priorities in his/her life. Misappropriation of one's priorities is exactly how secular concerns become the obstacle of effective leadership.

Not only should a leader be concerned about personal priorities, but also for those supervised. If workers you supervise are becoming consumed in secular concerns, they will always be divided in their attention. This hurts productivity and creativity immensely.

The Apostle Paul's instruction to Timothy in this regard is recorded in chapter 6. Paul deals with secular concerns as seen in attitude in the work place; secular concern when dealing with difficult people; and then secular concerns regarding financial freedom.

"All who are under the yoke of slavery should consider their masters worthy of full respect, so that God's name and our teaching may not be slandered. Those who have believing masters are not to show less respect for them because they are brothers. Instead, they are to serve them even better, because those who benefit from their services are believers, and dear to them. These are the things you are to teach and urge on them." 1 Timothy 6:1-2

THE WORK PLACE (ITSELF) AS A SECULAR CONCERN

The work place itself can often set up a tone that influences and attitude and hence, spur on its own bevy of secular concern.

An effective leader must work at, and then achieve a tone in the work place that helps people to have a positive attitude toward what they are doing. This requires the leader to personally acquire a positive attitude and upbeat out look toward the work place. **So goes the leader's attitude, so goes the attitude in the work place!**

Every leader must realize that **who you are is more important** than what you do.

If at any time you discover you are not the person you want to be, then simply begin to walk, talk, think, dress and act like the person you want to be--and you will become that person.

> # If you aren't the person you want to be—simply begin to walk, talk, think, dress and act like the person you want to be— and you will become them!

THE BOSS AN A SECULAR CONCERN

Whoever you answer to is your boss (at least for the purpose of this discussion). This is the person—or persons—you must respect to be an effective leader. The instruction from the Apostle Paul to Timothy is to consider this person as valuable (whether you like them or not). The illustration used is the idea of "slavery." This idea has in our culture is disturbing to say to least, but in a broader (and historical) context it does say something about our attitude toward those who supervise us.

Leaders who understand they not only supervise others but they are also supervised, is a more effective leader because they understand the ramification and impact of every interpersonal dynamic.

When a person submits, listens, and works hard his/her character is strengthened. This strength correlates to effective leadership. As we protect the good name of our leaders, develop a servant's heart, and monitor our attitude about those leaders who supervise, we increase our own capacity to lead!

YOUR COLLEAGUES AS A SECULAR CONCERN

The "yoke of slavery" could easily extend to include the co-worker. The original Greek word for (yoke) is "zuggs" which means "to couple together" with one another.

People are "coupled together" in the work place on a regular basis. Most of the time you have no input as to those with whom you are "coupled together." On a regular basis, you are exposed to someone you don't know, don't like, or don't get along with. All kinds of difficulties can develop through competition, conflicts, or even personalities differences. Many people struggle with their co-workers—whether on the line at a factory—a teacher in the room next to you—or middle managers leading hundreds of people.

What has to happen for your relationship with a colleague to succeed is one simple thing—consider them valuable. Think of them as valuable, speak of them valuable, and talk to them as a person of value. This will change and maintain the positive kind of attitude necessary to remove the obstacle of secular concern to effective leadership.

Treat People as Valuable!

THE ATTITUDE OF THE WORK PLACE AS A SECULAR CONCERN

Always work hard! Hard work has a way of changing everything. Problems (secular concerns) dissolve if leaders concern themselves less with the little things and resolve to do their jobs and work hard.

Most of the distractions that happen—happen as a result of people not doing their work. A leader will become acutely discouraged if all he/she does is try to motivate those they supervise. Instead of trying so hard to motivate—lead by example—work hard yourself—they will notice.

DIFFICULT PEOPLE AS A SECULAR CONCERN

"If anyone teaches false doctrines and does not agree to the sound instruction of our Lord Jesus Christ and to godly teaching, he is conceited and understands nothing. He has an unhealthy interest in controversies and arguments that result in envy, quarreling, malicious talk, evil suspicions and c onstant friction b etween men o f c orrupt m ind, w ho have been robbed of the truth and who think that godliness is a means to financial gain." 1 Timothy 6:3-5

Difficult people are often a n obstacle to effective leadership. Who the difficult person is often varies. Some people are difficult for everyone to deal with, while others are specific to the leader's personality—one can get along with many others except maybe one or two people.

The instruction the Apostle Paul give Timothy may not be all-inclusive, it does give us some important applications:

100

1. **There may be some people with whom you may never get along.**

Don't carry guilt over personality conflicts. Let it go. So many times we futilely try to do our best with a certain person. Things go well for a while then something happens—and you try again to please them. This kind of cycle is not good—for you or for them! If the leader gets used to having conflict—then feeling guilt—having conflict—then feeling guilt—there becomes a "dependency" on this kind of pain.

There may be some people with whom you won't ever get along. Don't allow yourself to feel smarter or better than someone else. Neither allow yourself to feel less than someone else. When you feel conflicted with difficult people simply accept it for what it is—because—**"it is what it is!"** Doing more (or less) will cause you to be constantly frustrated—that means you won't be the effective leader you need to be.

2. **There are some people from whom you should just stay away.**

Paul's instruction to Timothy is to stay away from those who love to argue or create controversy. Our human make-up was never created for arguments and controversy. God created us to live in a garden—or at least the emotional level of living in a garden.

> # We weren't created (or built) to live under the stress we do today.

3. There may be people who are deceiving you (have you "buffaloed") right now!

There is a two fold test to use in determining if a person is deceiving you:

- **Is this person truthful?** Truthfulness tells much more than a person just trying to cover their bases—it tells us who they are—their character. Anyone who lies has to tell another one to cover up the one they just told.

  Have you heard them tell an untruth? If you have— they will lie to you as well.

  Finally, don't make excuses for people who don't tell the truth. A half truth is still a lie. Not telling the entire story when you have a chance to, is a lie. You don't have to make a big deal out of it—just file it in your mind and remember that this person is not a truth-teller. Don't trust them.

- **Is this person doing it just for the money?** If you discover that someone you supervise is doing their job just for the money—there may be something happening that you may never discover: This person is also deceiving you at different levels.

  If a person has money as their center, they will keep this job (at whatever cost) until another source of income develops. If it continues, you will find yourself not being able get to the bottom of things in helping people to develop.

An effective leader doesn't over-react when discovering the deception in the ranks. They simply learn who to trust and who not to trust—thereby building the organization on solid people.

THE SECULAR CONCERN OF FINANCIAL FREEDOM

"But godliness with contentment is great gain. For we brought nothing into the world, and we can take nothing out of it—but if we have food and clothing, we will be content with that. People who want to get rich fall into temptation and a trap and into many foolish and harmful desires that plunge men into ruin and destruction. For the love of money is the root of all kinds of evil. Some people, eager for money, have wandered from the faith, and pierced themselves with many griefs." 1 Timothy 6:6-10

The Apostle Paul gives Timothy some instructions that originate from a deeply spiritual perspective. Effective leaders apply these deeply spiritual concepts through synthesizing them into attitude and approach. Truly spiritual ideas are never "spiritualized" but rather applied—constantly seen, but never "heard."

The most effective leader is the one who leads through love not because they "have too." The "have too" mentality is because of a need for the money (generally speaking the supervisor is paid more than those supervised). If someone supervises because they need the money, rather than because they are gifted to lead—the leadership will never be effective.

Effective leaders are financially free. What does "financial freedom" mean? The Apostle Paul brings clarity to the idea of

103

financial freedom in the life of the effective leader. Paul's teachings are not what you would normally hear—and it isn't exactly what you would want to hear—but the Apostle Paul's idea of financial freedom is attainable for any leader who desires to be effective!

> # Godliness with contentment
> # is great gain.

This one statement "godliness with contentment is great gain" is actually all the truth necessary for every leader to be financially free.

Financial bondage is obviously prevalent in our organizations. People never really achieve their potential because of their worries and concerns about their living and financial bondage. The idea of "godliness" should change all that.

"Godliness" means the entire gospel scheme—including the birth by a virgin, a sinless life, death, burial, resurrection, **AND my involvement in the proclamation of this gospel scheme.**

"Contentment" is the idea that what I have right now is what I supposed to have right now—I understand that, am freed by that, and am satisfied with that. Further:

- The job I have right now is the job I am supposed to have.
- The career I have right now is the career I am supposed to have.
- The financial situation I have right now is the financial situation I am supposed to have.

When a leader combines the idea that I participate in the gospel scheme in my daily life, with the idea that I am where I am supposed to be right now, what develops is a powerfully effective leader who understands the purpose of his/her career is having a **great impact on the life of others—which is the greatest goal of any endeavor.**

When a leader experiences the insight of godliness, it creates the greatest kind of freedom imaginable.

Financial freedom is achieved, not by a degree of wealth, but by a degree of the heart. When you attain the realization that your impact for Christ is the greatest achievement possible—financial freedom (freedom period) is yours!

Be content with the basics!

Paul's second idea directs us back to the basics—food to eat, and clothes to wear. These are the basics with which we should be content.

All of our needs and wants expand from these basics. We become frustrated, not because our basics aren't covered, but when someone else gets something you don't. Our materialistic society norms have become askew. Our appetites, desires, and drives cause us to expand our wants into aggressive desire. Soon we become frustrated, resentful and angry.

There are many different formulas, plans, and strategies for people to achieve the life they always wanted. We are told "you can do anything you set your mind to." The problem is, we set our minds on the wrong thing. When you set your mind on a "thing you want" you lose the basic sense of freedom—because you fall into the bondage of that "thing" desired.

A leader who is driven toward excess, especially in personal material accomplishments, make selfish decisions, not decisions in the best interest of the organization. A leader who is self-absorbed is not only not effective, but dangerous in many respects. The key to freedom is not a materialistic drive, but an organizational excellence drive.

Avoid the trap!

Paul warned the most basic trap of life is the pursuit if getting rich. Tragically, the most harmful motive you can have in your work or in your life is to do well just so that you will be rewarded financially. Too often, in our society, we have seen the heartbreak and emptiness of those who have ruined their lives in the pursuit of gaining "richness."

Being "rich" does not necessarily mean money. Rich (plouteo) literally means "to be increased with goods." As material as it sounds, it is actually a mind set or mentality.

God created the world to multiply—to reproduce. Our mentality needs to be that of multiplication. Financial freedom means that I no longer am in bondage to money. Instead, I have learned to avoid the trap of being pulled into the drive toward materialism—I have learned that when God increases my life **everything is included!**

106

The better you do—the better you will do. If a leader decides to make the work of leadership and the drive to lead effectively the goal in one's life and career—there will always be plenty of material resources. Let your skill pursue the money—don't learn a skill to get money.

We do our best and let God increase our lives. He knows what we need, when we need it, and what is best for us.

Stay God centered!

The reason that finances become the center of our lives is because it is becomes the focus of all our striving. Everyone looks forward to payday with great excitement, but it is important to stay so centered on God that payday is just like any other day. The purpose for work needs to be to serve God and others, not to obtain more possessions.

The striving after things is a worthless endeavor, because enough is never enough.

A leader needs to accept the fact that God will take care of him/her. Even if the people the leader works for are extremely cheap, God will still multiply the leader in every area of life, not just financially.

We need to look past the person who signs the paycheck as the provider. The person who signs your paycheck is only an instrument in God blessing your life. Regardless of your job or organization, the effective leader sees him/herself as working for God and their resources come from God. Seeing God as your source is a huge part of living and leading a life that is

God centered. It is also becomes the bottom line for removing secular concerns as an obstacle to effective leadership.

> "For we brought nothing into the world, and we can take nothing out of it—but if we have food and clothing, we will be content with that."
>
> --Paul

QUESTIONS FOR DISCUSSION

1. How would define "secular concerns" as it relates to being an obstacle to effective leadership? _____

_____
_____
_____

2. How can the work place itself be an obstacle to effective leadership? _____

_____
_____
_____

3. Share some ways you can deal with difficult people.

_____
_____
_____
_____

4. Do you know people who love to argue and stir things up? How have you dealt with them? How should you deal with them? _____

_____
_____

5. What are the 2 ways to test if someone could be deceiving you right now? _____

_____
_____

6. What does "godliness with contentment" mean? What does it mean to you? _____

_____
_____
_____

OBSTACLE #7
Losing the Edge

"Edge" is a term used to conceptualize being at your optimum and at the same time enjoying what you do. Many times leaders either aren't enjoying their work or aren't experiencing success.

"Living on the edge" is the affirmation of being at your optimum and enjoying what you do. It can be seen (and felt) in the life of a leader through things like—

- **A person who loves/cares for others.**

- **A genuine feeling of satisfaction in one's life and work.**

- **A personal life that is free from guilt.**

- **A conscience that is clear.**

Every effective leader's desire is to keep the edge in their life. If a leader has no interest in being at his/her optimum—the edge has already been lost!

The Apostle Paul closes his first letter of instruction to Timothy with personal hints in keeping a sharp edge. Verses 11 through 16 in chapter 6 develop the strategy to keep the edge. Verses 17 through 19 changed the thought to sharpening the edge.

This instruction gives invaluable insight in how to keep your edge—regardless of what you do.

"But you, man of God, flee from all this, and pursue righteousness, godliness, faith, love, endurance and gentleness. Fight the good fight of faith. Take hold of the eternal life to which you were called when you made your good confession in the presence of many witnesses. In the sight of God, who gives life to everything, and of Christ Jesus, who while testifying before Pontius Pilate made the good confession, I charge you to keep this commandment without spot or blame until the appearing of our Lord Jesus Christ, which God will bring about in his own time— God, the blessed and only ruler, the King of kings and Lord of lords, who alone is immortal and who lives in unapproachable light, whom no one has seen or can see. To him be honor and might forever. Amen." 1 Timothy 6:11-16

1st Part of the Strategy in Keeping Your Edge: <u>FLEE</u>

The word "flee" is a fairly animated term—but it gets our attention enough to listen.

We need to flee from those things that we know cause us to become distracted and disoriented. We need to make the right choices. It is with in our own power and will to be self-controlled.

Every leader learns every day a little more about themselves. The more you know—the better equipped you are to avoid (flee from) those things that would cause you to lose your edge—those things that would cause you not to enjoy your life, or not allow you to succeed, or both.

The idea of "fleeing" is not the same thing as running from something. It is not running in fear if you realize where you are weak or have a capacity to lose your edge—it is being wise and avoiding those things.

2ND Part of the Strategy in Keeping Your Edge: PURSUE

If you are "fleeing" you should also be "pursuing" something else. "Pursue" or the reach toward something should be so designed that effective leaders have a personal challenge that will help them grow professionally.

Unless a leader sets a direction for something, there will never really be anything you are pursuing. If you are fleeing from things that distract you to keep you from losing your edge, here are some things to pursue (for/with the same purpose):

- **Righteousness**—Free yourself up from things that pollute your mind and fill it up with positive things that help you.

- **Faith Building**—Practice turning things over to God. Entrusting your life to God is as much as an exercise in building yourself as exercise is to your body.

- **Love**—Concentrate on being kind toward everyone. Especially center kindness on people who are not kind.

- **Endurance**—Train yourself to stick with it until finished. Further, don't just "stick with it" but excel while you are sticking with it. Don't just finish— finish well.

- **Gentleness**—Understanding the needs of people. Don't make assumptions or take things for granted. Learn to listen to people and their needs.

3rd Part of the Strategy in Keeping Your Edge:

FIGHT THE GOOD FIGHT

The "fight" with regard to a strategy of keeping your edge, is the idea of staying true to your convictions.

What are your convictions? What things do you believe in? What is it you are opposed to? What things are right? What things are wrong?

Every leader must come to terms with their convictions.

Convictions should be embraced as a friend, not an enemy of the effective leader. Our convictions help guide us in normal times, but especially in times of indecision, confusion, and disorientation.

4th Part of the Strategy in Keeping Your Edge:

THINK ABOUT ETERNITY AT LEAST ONE TIME PER DAY.

When a leader is only thinking about the "here and now" the bar is set too low. Thinking about eternity and one's place in it helps a leader to understand that life larger than our momentary circumstances.

A leader needs to be empowered for the moment and feel the success and enjoyment that comes in their work—but in case a person gets to feeling too good about personal success, a leader needs to see the world from a larger view.

Thinking about eternity is simply allowing the challenges of life to become small in comparison to the awesomeness of the eternal realm.

5th Part of the Strategy in Keeping Your Edge:

<u>DECLARE YOUR INTENTION—MAKE YOUR COMMITMENT KNOWN.</u>

An effective leader must declare his/her intention to keep the edge.

This strategy means an effective leader declares their intention specifically:

"I, (your name) intend to operate my life at an optimum level and at the same time enjoy myself!"

"Command those who are rich in this present world not to be arrogant nor to put their hope in wealth, which is so uncertain, but to put their hope in God, who richly provides us with everything for our enjoyment. Command them to do good, to be rich in good deeds and to be generous and willing to share. In this way they will lay up treasure for themselves as a firm foundation for the coming age, so that they may take hold of the life that is truly life." 1 Timothy 6:17-19

Keeping your edge requires an occasional "sharpening" of it. More than "required maintenance" the idea of sharpening your edge (running at your optimum and enjoying yourself) means growth is needed in your life.

The Apostle Paul gives Timothy some ways to develop growth in his life and thereby continue living on the edge:

- **Everything God has provided is for us to enjoy.** Enjoying God's provision requires us to put our hope and trust in Him. This idea will keep an effective leader sharp. Many people begin to look at the work of their hands and put their hope and trust in themselves. When this begins to happen to leaders, they run the potential risk of losing their edge.

- **Do valuable things with your time.** Before jumping into any endeavor an effective leader will examine its value.

- **Be rich in good deeds.** The richer we are in good deeds, the sharper our edge will be—the lack of good deeds dulls our edge.

- **Meet the needs of others.** The idea the Apostle Paul uses of "imparting" shows a personal involvement in the meeting of the needs of others.

- **Stay sharp with your communication skills.** Communication is the key to being at your optimum. The sharper you are with communication, the sharper you make edge.

STAYING SHARP

"Timothy, guard what has been entrusted to your care. Turn away from godless chatter and opposing ideas of what is falsely called knowledge, which some have professed and in so doing have wandered from the faith." 1Timothy 6: 20-21

In the Apostle Paul's closing remarks in his first letter to Timothy, he delivers three quick (and emphatic) imperatives on how to stay sharp.

<u>**Guard the trust people place in you like it is something deeply sacred!**</u> Valuing and guarding trust is vitally important. You should not take lightly, pass off easily, or ignore it when someone places trust in you. Whether just a little trust, or a lot of trust—it is all sacred.

<u>**Avoid using empty words or giving attention to them when you hear others using them.**</u> Staying sharp requires us to watch the words we use. Conversations between people are very important. Conversations build trust—or they destroy trust depending on the words people use.

<u>**Stay true to yourself.**</u> Keep a clear conscience close as a valuable treasure. Apologize when you need too—don't fall on your sword just to make people happy. **Be honest with YOU.**

QUESTIONS FOR DISCUSSION

1. How do you define "the edge" as it relates to your life? How would it apply to your life? _____

    _____
    _____
    _____

2. From what do you know you need to "flee"? What are some things you know you need to "pursue?"

    _____
    _____
    _____
    _____

3. What does it mean to "fight the good fight?" _____

    _____
    _____

4. How does meeting the needs of others apply to your life? Your leadership? _____

    _____
    _____
    _____
    _____

5. How would you define "godless chatter?" _____

    _____
    _____
    _____

OBSTACLE #8
Lack of Consistency

Often referred to as "the miracle of compound interest" there is an investment ideal that brings illustrates the next obstacle to effective leadership. The idea of—**"it's not how much, but how often"**—sums up the how consistency works for savings and investing. More importantly, this concept of powerful simple consistent habits of saving/investment can be applied in your personal life.

Consistency in your personal life extends into your professional life as well. Consistency in leadership is essential to being effective—and is a horrible load to bear if a leader is inconsistent.

In the first chapter of his second letter to Timothy, the Apostle Paul deals with three areas of consistency—in personal things, in public things, and in difficult things.

The whole idea of **"it's not how much, but how often"** under girds everything we see in Paul's letter regarding consistency.

CONSISTENCY IN PERSONAL THINGS

"Paul, an apostle of Christ Jesus by the will of God, according to the promise of life that is in Christ Jesus, to Timothy my dear son: Grace, mercy and peace from God the Father and Christ Jesus our Lord. I thank God, whom I serve, as m y f orefather did, w ith a clear c onscience, as night and day I constantly remember you in my prayers. Recalling your tears, I l ong to see you, so t hat I may be filled with joy. I have been reminded of your sincere faith, which first lived in your grandmother Lois and your

mother Eunice and I am persuaded now lives in you also. For this reason I remind you to fan into flame the gift of God which is in you through the laying on of my hands. For God did not give us a spirit of timidity, but a spirit of power, of love and of self-discipline." 2 Timothy 1:1-7

The first benchmark when dealing with consistency for a leader—is the leader's consistency in daily prayers

---

The very first illustration we see in Paul's writings that draws our attention to consistency in personal things is prayer. The Apostle Paul's testimony is that he remembers them constantly in prayer.

A consistent prayer life is a powerful tool for an effective leader. On the other hand, a lack of a prayer life can be an obstacle to effective leadership.

The key to a consistent prayer life is developing a habit that becomes a behavior. A leader should set up a schedule of 4 to 5 times a day to offer prayers—which develops the mentality that the leader is always in an attitude or spirit of prayer all the time throughout the day.

A leader needs to take conscience times out of the day to focus on God and offer one's thoughts to Him. The leader must also believe that when the conscience time is ended that the spirit of prayer remains.

Every effective leader commits the entire day to God, but is in constant contact with God through prayer. Consistency in this way will root out a couple of unbecoming behaviors.

First, whining and complaining will leave your life if you are in a spirit of prayer—because you can't be complaining about something and praying about it at the same time. The two are just not compatible with one another. You will do one or the other.

Second, if you develop a consistent prayer life, criticism will not be present in your life. The logic is—you can't be praying about something and criticizing it at the same time.

Remember when it comes to your prayer life as a leader: **"It's not how much, but how often."**

The second benchmark when dealing with consistency for a leader—is the leader's family issues.

The Apostle Paul gives the example of Timothy's own family as that of consistency. What a person does in the home will revisit for generations to come. What is consistently sown will be reaped for years to come. This includes the bad as well as the good. Unfortunately, most parents don't realize this until it is too late.

Most leaders become consumed in their work load. The amount of time at work can become an object of acute guilt—which is not positive. This kind of guilt can cause a leader to become personally defensive when relating with the family. No doubt leaders have to work hard, long hours, but don't forget when it comes to family issues: **"It's not how much, but how often."**

A simplified family pattern is always the best. Be simple in your rules—simple in their understanding. Be a good example of lifestyle and your family will follow. Instill with in your family the benefits of consistency.

There may be some healing that needs to take place in your family. It is never too late for reconciliation. Open up the issues and then give it time to heal. Whatever you do—start being consistent. **It is never too late—there is always a point of correction when you begin to become consistent in any area.**

Sometimes the leader will have to seek forgiveness from his/her family. You may even have to deal with secret sins in your life. Remember that people and situations can change. **"It is not how much, but how often."**

> **The third benchmark when dealing with consistency for a leader—is the leader's spiritual life.**

The Apostle Paul declares we are not given a spirit of fear. We don't need to fear—but fear often keeps us from being consistent. Paul emphasizes three areas we for consistency:

1. **The use of our energy.** We need to find good behaviors to use our energy. Our energy is our life. It needs to be invested into conduct that will multiply our effectiveness.

2. **Kindness.** Beginning at midnight every night every single p erson i s g iven 8 6,400 o f these little things t o use as we please. At midnight the next night they are all done in. Don't worry—we get a new supply every night—and this happens over and over, again and again. H ave y ou f igured it o ut? We r eceive 8 6,400 seconds of time every single day to be used as we please. An important key in the investment of these is if you allow every one of them to be filled with kindness toward others.

3. **Self Control.** We are to be consistently self controlled. One deviation from this directive can cause irreconcilable damage to character, life, family or future. Self control should come easily to an effective leader because that is an essential characteristic in leadership. A leader often has to restrain him/herself from saying or doing what they would really like to say or do. A leader's family deserves this kind of restraint as well. A leader's family should not be treated worse than the leader treats those they supervise. Frustration and disappointment in the work place should not be taken out on the family. This behavior is a sign of a lack of self control.

CONSISTENCY IN PUBLIC THINGS

Consistency in public life doesn't mean to be a "show boat." Consistency in public is natural reflection of consistency in private. We must be consistent in our private lives first—and our public lives will follow.

"So do not be ashamed to testify about our Lord, or ashamed of me his prisoner. But join with me in suffering for the gospel, by the power of God, who has saved us and called us to a holy life—not because of anything we have done but because of his own purpose and grace. This grace was given in Christ Jesus before the beginning of time, but it has now been revealed through the appearing of our Savior Christ Jesus, who has destroyed death and has brought life and immortality to light through the gospel. And of this gospel I was appointed a herald and an apostle and a teacher. That is why I am suffering as I am. Yet I am not ashamed, because I know w hom I have b elieved, and am convinced that he is able to guard what I have entrusted to him for that day." 1 Timothy 2:8-12

<u>**"I know whom I have believed"**</u> is the start to consistency in your public life—it is—who owns you? To whom does your life belong?

We are often quick to answer that our life belongs to God, but the most essential aspect of God's ownership of your life is how much of your leadership does God own? Unless it all belongs to God in a practical, daily way it isn't true!

<u>**"I am persuaded"**</u> means that I am convinced. Effective leaders can't convince others of something unless they first believe the truth themselves.

People are looking for a sincere leader. The most basic level of sincerity is in a person who believes something for themselves before pushing it on others.

"That He is able to guard what I have entrusted to Him" means that there are many things we don't understand. Yet, despite my lack of understanding, I still believe in the one to whom I have entrusted the things I don't understand.

No leader is ever going to be able to "figure it all out." That is why it is so important to believe God is at work even when we don't feel Him, see Him, or understand the circumstances.

Every leader has "blind spots" in their leadership. Knowing that you have entrusted yourself to God's care will help to navigate during those times of disorientation and confusion.

No leader is ever able to "figure it all out"—nor should you feel like you have to!

CONSISTENCY IN DIFFICULT TIMES

The true test of consistency comes during the tough and difficult times. In his teaching to Timothy, the Apostle Paul uses some personal examples to illustrate that point.

"What you have heard from me, keep as a pattern of sound teaching, with faith and love in Christ Jesus. Guard the

good deposit that was entrusted to you—guard it with the help of the Holy Spirit who lives in us. You know that everyone in the province of Asia has deserted me, including Phygelus and Hermogenes. May the Lord show mercy to the household of Onesiphorus, because he often refreshed me and was not ashamed of my chains. On the contrary, when he was in Rome, he searched hard for me until he found me. May the Lord grant that he will find mercy from the Lord on that day! You know very well in how many ways he helped me in Ephesus." 2 Timothy 1:13-18

Consistency in a person's life is like saving for a rainy day. The longer your pattern of consistent behavior has been, the more likely you are to stay consistent during difficult times.

The Apostle Paul was one person whose example is a solid illustration of the consistent life. When Paul served on the Sanhedrin Council he was consistent in all ways as a Hebrew leader—after his conversion to Christ he was a consistent Christian leader. Consistency in life is in the deepest manner an important character attribute. The lack of consistency is a major obstacle in a person's life—and especially to effective leadership.

Whether or not a person stays consistent in private life, public life, or in difficult times depends primarily on an effective leader's resolve to remove inconsistency from their life.

> # Consistency in life is hard work for everyone!

QUESTIONS FOR DISCUSSION

1. How do you define consistency in your private life? Public life? _____

   _____

   _____

   _____

2. In what areas of your life do you need to remove inconsistency? _____

   _____

   _____

   _____

3. How do you apply "it's not how much, but how often" to areas of your life? _____

   _____

   _____

   _____

   _____

4. How would a consistent prayer life help a person become an effective leader? _____

   _____

   _____

   _____

5. What are we given 86,400 of every day? _____

6. Explain: "I know whom I have believed." _____

   _____

   _____

   _____

   _____

   _____

   _____

   _____

OBSTACLE #9
Living an Unbalanced Life

Leaders display various amounts of intensity. Leadership often requires a leader to become intense because of the focus, attention and energy required for many of the tasks of leadership.

Just as common as intensity in the life of the leader is the lack of intensity in the life of those he/she supervises. The same thing can be said in the personal/family life of the leader. The leader brings intensity into the home because that is how he/she is "geared" all day.

The difference between the intensity of a leader and the lack of intensity in those around him/her creates a frustration that enhances an imbalance. The leader will often react to the lack of intensity as people "not caring" or a lack of passion for their tasks or responsibilities. This reaction usually surfaces by the leader's pep talks; in committee meetings; and often through a leader's life in general going out of balance.

Leaders often fall into the idea that they can motivate people. Although motivation is possible, a leader with any intensity at all begins to believe he/she can motivate anyone. **The intensity in the leader's life blinds him/her to the fact that many people are not able to be motivated!**

Another example of unbalanced living can be seen when a leader takes up a "cause" he/she believe in. The intense spirit of the leader creates the attitude that everyone should feel as strongly about the cause as they do personally. Rarely is a leader able to realize that he/she shouldn't expect others to be as committed to their personal cause. Often the leader experiences into huge emotional swings—that he/she hides from others. The leader feel confused and rejected but instead of opening up and dealing the feelings and the intensity—and emotionally gets turned upside down and creates an imbalanced life.

An effective leader must live a balanced life. Balanced living requires determined concentration. It is through the balanced life that we are of the most use to those we lead.

Tangents, causes, radical approaches, and intensity don't serve the best interest of effective leadership. Balanced living does.

The Apostle Paul in his second letter to Timothy brings out twelve penetrating principles of removing imbalance from our lives.

PRINCIPLE #1:
PROPOGATION MINDED

"You then, my son, be strong in grace that is in Christ Jesus. And the things you have heard me say in the presence of many witnesses entrust to reliable men who will also be qualified to teach others." 2 Timothy 2:1-2

Effective leaders realize they are doing their part in the process of life. They do their best and pass on what they know. They teach and train others. They leave things better then they found them.

The way to retain a balanced life is to see yourself as a part of the puzzle—a piece of the total. Imbalance comes when leaders begin to think they are carrying the whole mantel. No one can carry a responsibility like that and retain a balanced life! No one is intended to carry that large of a load—it is really self-induced. The resulting leadership dynamic will be a complete lack of effectiveness because people won't be able to follow their leader.

The Apostle Paul is an example of someone who poured his life into his pupil—Timothy. Paul's vision was that Timothy would eventually replace Paul as an apostolic leader. The entire purpose of these two letters to Timothy was to teach and train a young man to carry on—to carry the mantel. Paul makes it clear to Timothy that this "mantel" is not too large. Further, Paul makes it clear that life needs to stay in balance or you won't have anyone left to lead.

As you find those you can come along side, train, and mentor to eventually replace you, Paul gives three directives we should use in our instruction:

1. **Stay Strong.** Strength comes from God. Paul wants Timothy to keep himself balanced—and that will help him stay strong.

2. **Listen—and teach others to listen.** Listening doesn't come naturally—it is deliberately acquired. Anyone interested in living and leading a balanced life must be a listener. Any thing you need in your life can be achieved not through personal intensity, but through listening.

3. **Look for reliable people.** Don't pour yourself into dishonest people—people who don't listen—people

who aren't consistent—or people who can't keep a confidence.

Effective leaders don't just sit around and soak it all in—they learn so they can share and mentor others! Sharing life's lessons as well as business concepts, provides us with the position to stay balanced in our thinking and in our lives.

PRINCIPLE #2:
ENDURE ALL THE LIFE CYCLES

"Endure hardship with us like a good soldier of Christ Jesus." 2 Timothy 2:3

We are constantly analyzing the events happening to us and around us using various measures of impact. Our reaction to the situations in which we find ourselves varies depending on circumstance, situation, personality, and dynamic.

Whatever the situation—every effective leader knows that everything in life is cyclical. The best we can do sometimes is simply endure the current cycle—because "this too will pass."

There is no way to adequately prepare for some of the cycles of life. That is why the best way to prepare for life is to prepare for the cycle. Realizing that life comes in cycles goes a long to in living a balanced life.

The truth is: If things are going bad—hold on—things will get better. Are things going good for you? Just wait—things will get tough sometime soon. Why? Life comes and goes in cycles. We must endure every cycle.

PRINCIPLE #3:
WISE INVOLVEMENT

"No one serving as a soldier gets involved in civilian affairs—he wants to please his commanding officer." 2 Timothy 2:4

Nothing hurts the balance in life more than unwise involvement. The text gives us an excellent directive and illustration in this matter. The soldier should not get involved in areas which would involve a compromise of principle or integrity.

A leader's own peer group can often take you to places you never thought you would go. Whether a certain way to dress, place to eat, or car to drive—one's peers have a tremendous influence on many things a leader does.

An effective leader is single-minded in the area one's involvements. There are no compromises of integrity or character allowed. These compromises start when one allows involvement to compromise their conviction, principles, or standards of conduct.

A leader should always step up and answer a question before getting involved in anything. **Does what I have been asked to** involve compromise in my values, standards, or beliefs in any way?

Influential leaders have to constantly fight the urge to get involved in everything. People who can influence others are highly sought after to become involved in many worthy causes—but unwise involvements or over involvement have a tendency to cause people to become unbalanced in their leadership.

PRINCIPLE #4:
UNDERSTANDING THE RULES

"Similarly, if anyone competes as an athlete he does not receive the victor's crown unless he competes according to the rules." 2 Timothy 2:5

It is interesting to note the Apostle Paul's emphasis is on the rules—not the race, not the speed, not the competition—but the rules of the race.

Often we get so caught up in the race (and winning it) that we forget about the rules. It is everything else about the race that causes us to lose our balance—except for the rules—but normally it is everything else over which we obsess.

"Rules" can sometimes be vague—the unspoken, yet implied kind of thing. Other times they are written out by the time clock—or in memo form sent out through email.

Understanding the rules requires four important things:

1. **Whatever it takes—find out what the rules are.**

2. **Understand the rules as you analyze them.**

3. **Play by the rules you know.**

4. **Adjust yourself from time to time—sometimes the rules change—stay up to date.**

PRINCIPLE #5:
HARD WORK

"The hardworking farmer should be the first to receive a share of the crops." 2 Timothy 2:6

Anyone who lives a balanced life has to be a hard worker because just trying to live a balanced life is hard work!

The discipline and consistency required through working hard is reward enough, but hard work creates a blessing and multiplication in one's life.

Every effective leader is a hard worker. People around you know it—those you supervise will emulate it as you model it.

PRINCIPLE #6:
GENERATIONAL MENTALITY

"Reflect on what I am saying, for the Lord will give you insight into all this. Remember Jesus Christ, raised from the dead, descended from David. This is my gospel, for which I am suffering even to the point of being chained like a criminal. But God's word is not chained. Therefore I endure everything for the sake of the elect, that they too may obtain salvation that is in Christ Jesus, with eternal glory. Here is a trustworthy saying: If we died with him, we will also reign with him. If we disown him, he will also disown us; if we are faithless he will remain faithful, for he cannot disown himself." 2 Timothy 2:7-13

Generational mentality is the idea that decisions made today are based upon what is the best for the people who will be living in the future.

This kind of attitude is the ultimate idea of balanced living. Rather than making decisions based upon short term gratification (which have the tendency to make us unbalanced) we will make decisions that delay the gratification for later.

Making decisions based on the generations to come ends up taking our vision out of a tunnel and boasts it to a higher level of thinking and understanding.

As a leader, ask yourself—**how will this decision affect my children and my children's children?** Let your answer be the thing that balances you in decision making!

Generational mentality will ultimately be the thought process that prevents a leader from becoming self-absorbed. A leader who is thinking of others rarely ever makes a selfish decision. One who is thinking about the generations to come never thinks in terms of what is the best "for me."

PRINCIPLE #7:
DON'T GET CAUGHT UP IN THE SMALL STUFF.

"Keep reminding them of these things. Warn them before God against quarreling about words; it is of no value, and only ruins those who listen." 2 Timothy 2:14

Imbalance is created in one's life when all the small stuff finally mounts up and you can't take the pressure from it. Whether it is quarreling, discussions, criticism, or pickiness—small things can throw a leader quickly out of balance.

Anything that causes a leader to lose focus should be categorized as "small stuff."

The Apostle Paul indicates it is our responsibility to warn people about the tendency to get caught up in small stuff. We can not sit on the sidelines and be passive. Jumping in and helping people avoid the small stuff will help to keep us balanced.

PRINCIPLE #8:
ONE STEP AT A TIME

"Do your best to present yourself to God as one approved, a workman who does not need to be ashamed and who correctly handles the word of truth." 2 Timothy 2:15

Everything has a progression. First you lie in a cradle, acquire the ability to roll over, then crawl, and eventually walk. The same thing is true in leadership.

No one ever really "arrives" in life or in leadership because we are always learning something. Sometimes we feel we have to project a larger image to others than what we really are. All this kind of thinking (and leading) does is cause your life to go out of balance.

The balanced life takes everything one step at a time—and—**enjoys each step you take!**

PRINCIPLE #9:
BE POSITIVE

"Avoid godless chatter, because those who indulge in it will become more and more ungodly. Their teaching will spread like gangrene. Among them are Hymenaeus and Philetus, who have wandered away from the truth. They

say that the resurrection has already taken place, and they destroy the faith of some. Never the less, God's solid foundation stands firm, sealed with this inscription: The Lord knows those who are his, and everyone who confesses the name of the Lord must turn away from wickedness." 2 Timothy 2: 16-19

"Godless chatter" in this context can be interpreted as negative talking. This is especially emphasized in the phrase, "their talking is like gangrene."

Negative thinking and talking should be treated like a highly infectious, and deadly, disease. It causes leadership to become askew and imbalanced in approach.

Leaders who become negative tend to continually come across angry. People who you supervise will become confused and unproductive under a negative leader.

Effective leaders target negative thinking and talk in their lives as unacceptable. They hold those around them accountable in the same regard.

PRINCIPLE #10
CONSTANTLY CLEANSING

"In a large house there are articles not only of gold and silver, but also of wood and clay; some are for noble purposes some for ignoble. If a man cleanses himself from the latter, he will be an instrument for noble purposes, made holy, useful to the Master and prepared to do any good work." 2 Timothy 2:20-21

A clean heart is essential to a balanced life. An effective leader pursues spiritual cleansing constantly. A person who wants to be an effective leader understands humans are flawed, but inner cleansing is important to overcome human frailty.

No one is perfect—but everyone should be cleansed constantly of their humanness.

The Apostle Paul uses a comparison between gold and silver verses wood and clay—things that last compared to things that don't. The difference in the human dynamic (and leadership endeavor) comes as we see our inner lives as important for lasting value. It is that part of ourselves that need to be constantly cleansed for vitality.

PRINCIPLE #11:
BE KIND

"Flee the evil desires of youth, and pursue righteousness, faith, love and peace, along with those who call on the Lord out of a pure heart. Don't have anything to do with foolish and stupid arguments, because you know they produce quarrels. And the Lord's servant must not quarrel; instead, he must be kind to everyone, able to teach, not resentful." 2 Timothy 2: 22-24

Kindness is a good foundation for anything—but especially good for living a balanced life.

A person who is kind is in complete control. Kindness is not always "sugar and spice and everything nice" because sometimes it involves being tough. Sometimes kindness means **NOT** giving someone something they want.

The spirit of kindness involves three things:

1. **Examine the facts of a situation.**

2. **Do the best thing for someone with the long term in mind.**

3. **Do whatever is necessary to do the above 2 things.**

PRINCIPLE #12:
ALWAYS TEACH

"Those who oppose him he must gently instruct, in the hope that God will grant them repentance leading them to a knowledge of the truth, and that they will come to their senses and escape from the trap of the devil, who has taken them captive to do his will." 2 Timothy 2: 25-26

An effective leader is both teachable and a teacher. **A leader is a teacher first because they should always be teaching.**

A teacher is someone who is teachable—who listens—and then passes it along. A teacher is well-prepared and organized. When a true teacher is present—so will trust be present in any situation. A leader is always a teacher!

QUESTIONS FOR DISCUSSION

1. What does "propagation mindedness" have to do with a balance life? _____

    _____

    _____

    _____

2. What is it we "endure?"_____

    _____

3. Why should a leader be wise in selecting their involvement? _____

    _____

    _____

    _____

4. What does it mean to "understand the rules?"____

    _____

    _____

5. What kinds of "small stuff" cause you to become distracted? _____

    _____

6. How does being positive (or being negative) relate to being balanced as a leader? _____

    _____

    _____

7. How do go about "constant cleansing" in your daily life? _____

    _____

    _____

OBSTACLE #10
Pride/Ego

An examination of obstacles to effective leadership would not be complete without looking at pride as an ego issue.

Pride is often the motivating force behind many of the activities a leader does without the needed accountability to keep the ego in check.

Pride and ego can be hidden and disguised so well that it isn't even recognizable. Further, pride can often be a self-justified behavior. Many advocate that pride is the impetus that causes us to do our best in our endeavors.

The Apostle Paul deals with pride as a problem that destroys the human character through a degenerative process. We are shown what it does to contribute a hurtful process—what it does at home—and then we are given help for our problem of pride.

PRIDE/EGO AND THE HUMAN CHARACTER

"But mark this: There will be terrible times in the last days. People will be lovers of themselves, lovers of money, boastful, proud, abusive, disobedient to their parents, ungrateful, unholy, without love, unforgiving, slanderous, without self-control, brutal, not lovers of good, treacherous, rash, conceited, lovers of pleasure rather than lovers of God—having a form of godliness but denying its power. Have nothing to do with them." 2 Timothy 3: 1-5

The concept of "last days" can mean any time but the reference to the end of times gives emphasis to the teaching. It is interesting to note that most of the Biblical references of the "last days" or "end of time" have to do with apocalyptic events—but in this case it has to do with human behaviors related to character.

Let's break down the ideas contained here and see how important it is for an effective leader to change.

Men will be lovers of self. "Lover of self" was a Greek term used to describe the person who not only thinks a lot of himself, but always put self first. People will develop such a confidence in themselves that they will see themselves as the center of everything that is happening. They will begin to believe that they are the most important entity among all the most important things.

When a leader begins to believe they are the most important thing, he/she will begin to lose leadership effectiveness. The more self absorbed the leader becomes, the less people will listen to the leader's direction. Associated with being self-centered is the terrible blind spot involved: A self absorbed leader is blind to the fact that no one is really following. So develops a slow and painful downward spiral.

Lovers of money. Nothing is a truer test of who a person is but by the use and attitude toward money. Look into a person's checkbook and you will see what he/she loves the most.

Money is only a tool and should always be considered in that manner.

The pride involved with money is omni-directional—a person could be prideful over having a lot of money—or—prideful over not having much of it.

An effective leader keeps money issues in balance. Money is the product of services rendered—so always be a servant first.

Boastful. Bragging, no matter what the context or circumstance, has no place in leadership. People will know who you are soon enough. They will find out what you have done on their own. They don't need to be reminded or told of your good works. When boastfulness occurs, it discounts considerably the effectiveness of the leader.

Arrogance. Feeling better than others or higher than others begins with stereotyping other people in the first place. No one should be placed in a category or in a box. Arrogant leaders are not effective in their leadership because they are never able to envision the potential in those they supervise.

Arrogant leaders never expect more from those they stereotype or box in. The predetermined attitude prevents the leader from seeing any more than first expected—even if there is a great deal more.

Abusive. In the context of leadership, abusiveness means to speak and stand against something. The reason abusiveness is consistent with the idea of pride/ego is people support only those things they have a part of and stand against those things in which they had no input. Everyone knows someone who is against anything they didn't think up themselves—this is the idea of "abusive" as it relates to pride/ego.

Leaders with an abusive attitude never effectively lead people. Those they supervise hold their breath and wait for them to leave. Why would people like this even have leadership positions? It happens all the time—those who put them into leadership positions haven't experienced this kind of abuse themselves and because pride is so easily disguised, the person appears like an effective leader.

Narrowness. The person controlled by their own pride is a narrow person. These narrow-minded people think only of themselves and how things will affect them. Their vision is one-sided and based upon how they see the issue. No one is able to persuade these people. Narrow-minded people are not open to study and research something out to see how others experienced a similar situation. Leaders who don't learn from others because of the narrowness that comes from their pride will never be effective leaders. No one can make every mistake—that is why we must quickly learn from other's mistakes and adapt things learned quickly. It also involves trusting the experience of others enough that we don't have to experience something personally to apply the lessons learned.

Unthankful. Unthankful people feel like the world owes them. This common problem creeps into a life unnoticed. Unthankfulness often happens when a person has dedicated themselves to an endeavor and feels like they haven't received recognition they deserve.

What develops is a gruesome cycle. No amount of recognition is enough for what the person feels like he deserves. No amount of money gives the person the value of what he/she feels has been invested. It is a miserable feeling for the person and makes everyone around the situation miserable as well. This attitude creates a negative work climate and environment.

Unholy. This concept does not mean irreligious, but wicked. Leadership driven by pride can sometimes manifest itself in ugly, wicked kinds of ways. Because people are afraid to confront the ugly treatment, this problem can go unchecked for quite some time.

Hardness. A pride filled leader lacks the compassion necessary to love others. This hardness is reflected in how a leader views his/her people. The hard hearted leader thinks if people would be more like him/her then everyone would be more successful.

Unforgiving. Unforgiveness has two dimensions in this concept. When looking at the pride of the leader, it means is a leader who goes back on their word. When this occurs, rarely does the person doing it ever realize and because of pride would never admit it. The second dimension is the actual lack of forgiveness for others. A leader who lacks forgiveness is constantly rehashing the mistakes of those they supervise—and bringing up past things.

Nothing will demoralize those you supervise faster than the reality that they will never be able to get past a mistake, a failure, or a simple mess-up.

Slanderous. An effective leader never accuses people. There is no point to spend your time bringing up things about others. What does that have to do with you anyway? The same amount of energy would be better invested removing the obstacle of pride/ego out of your life!

Self Control. A lack of self control is actually a problem with pride. The reason a person lacks control is because they think too much of self (pride).

Violence. Violence as an event is an extension of pride, but before the event is the violent talk. Effective leaders don't threaten people—because they don't have to. Threats and bullying may start in the school yard during recess, but those who do it continue to do so throughout life. It is pride. Leaders who threaten, bully, or intimidate those they supervise have missed essential development as a leader.

If you realize you are a "violent" leader you need to get pride/ego removed out of your life.

Despiser. The "despiser" is one who tends to be hostile. The despiser relates to pride this way: Anger that is justified becomes on going hostility. Perfectionism is often seen as the fruit of hostility derived from pride. Leaders who are perfectionist are a constant frustration to those they supervise—nothing they ever do is good enough.

Traitor. This is the leader whose pride motivates them to always be looking for the "next best deal" vocationally. A leader who is looking for the better job is obvious to those who work for him/her. An effective leader works hard at the place where God has opened the door—and will continue until God closes the door.

Indecisive. It is actually pride that causes a person to feel compelled to please others. The "pleaser personality" is afraid to do anything but make sure they keep others happy.

A pleaser person is usually indecisive. An effective leader is like being an umpire—you make the call—safe or out. Taking the best information available—the effective leader makes a decision and sticks by it.

Lovers of Pleasure. Leisure time and relaxation are necessary, but a person driven by pride has to outdo the pleasure they had the last time around. This kind of pleasure seeking doesn't keep boundaries—it is something that can rage out of control. A lover of pleasure leads people to their own prideful end.

These areas brought out by the Apostle Paul can be used as a check list for self improvement.

PRIDE/EGO AND THE HOME

"They are the kind who worm their way into homes and gain control over weak willed women, who are loaded down with sins and are swayed by all kinds of evil desires, always learning but never able to acknowledge the truth. Just as Jannes and Jambres opposed Moses, so also these men oppose the truth—men of depraved minds who as far as the faith is concerned are rejected. But they will not get very far because, as in the case of those men, their folly will be clear to everyone." 2 Timothy 3:6-9

Next, we are directed toward the home environment. There are some interesting perceptions brought out by the Apostle Paul's teaching in regard to pride as an obstacle to effective leadership.

PRIDE CREATES AN ATMOSPHERE OF JUSTIFICATION.

The person who is filled with pride is able to create his/her own justification about everything he/she does. Hypocrisy quickly develops because of justifying behavior.

Family pride is often developed through the family name. The family name is protected at any cost. Through this seemingly innocent situation, pride then worms its way throughout the home in various behaviors.

Pride often begins in the home as defense mechanisms—as an instinct for survival. Everyone has weak moments. It is in these weak moments that pride becomes an emotional dependency—it is what the weak use to help themselves be stronger. It is here that insecurity and inferiority can loom large, carefully disguised by pride.

There is no way a leader with these kinds of home issues with pride is every going to be able to be someone (or something) else in the workplace. An insecure leader who is masking it with pride—or a leader with an inferiority complex who is masking it with pride usually have a terrible home life. No one can keep his/her mask on forever.

If you want to see how effectively a person you are looking at will lead others, look no farther than their home!

PRIDE PROMPTS SIN

On the spiritual side of things—pride is sin. However, it doesn't just stop there—pride can create the atmosphere for many other sins as well.

149

Pride is like the wall of a decaying fortress—it requires constant work to reinforce the decay. The end result is pride creates and prompts great barriers of sin.

Insecurity creates a weakness in a person, so pride is used to replace and strengthen that weakness, which eventually leads to a fall as he/she become filled up with pride.

PRIDE CREATES "BLIND SPOTS"

Sadly, pride causes a major problem in a person's life—they are blinded to the truth. Since it is the truth that sets us free— these blind spots also create bondage because of the pride.

PRIDE MAKES PEOPLE LOOK FOOLISH

A general instruction to all of his students, the Apostle Paul often talked about dying daily to self. This was Paul's concept of not "swallowing pride" but dying to it!

A person who dies to pride in their life is not only preventing foolishness but also helping themselves in three key areas:

1. **A person who dies to pride is able to handle criticism—using it to become better at what they do.**

2. A person who dies to pride is better able to handle suggestions. The leader no longer has to be an authority on everything.

3. A person who dies to pride doesn't project an image or worry what people have to say about them.

PRIDE/EGO AND THE BIBLE

You, however, know all about my teachings, my way of life, my purpose, faith, patience, love, endurance, persecutions, sufferings—what kinds of things happened to me in Antioch, Iconium, and Lystra, the persecutions I endured. Yet the Lord rescued me from all of them. In fact, everyone who wants to live a godly life in Christ Jesus will be persecuted, while evil men and impostors will go from gad to worse, deceiving and being deceived. But as for you, continue in what you have learned and have become convinced of, because you know those from whom you learned it, and how from infancy you have known the Holy Scriptures, which are able to make you wise for salvation through faith in Christ Jesus. All Scripture is God-breathed a nd i s u seful for t eaching, rebuking, correcting, and training in righteousness. So that the man of God may be thoroughly equipped for every good work." 2 Timothy 3: 10-17

The Apostle Paul provides instruction for Timothy—and by extension—to every leader as to how to remove the obstacle of pride/ego from their life.

1. I must believe that the Bible is God's personal Word to me.

151

Anything less than God's personal Word means the Bible is just a nice story book. We must give the Bible its proper authority—and that being it has authority over MY life.

We must believe that the Bible applies personally, or we will forever be applying it to others—forgetting how it applies to me.

When one begins to believe the Bible was written for me—that it applies to me personally—there will be no end to the challenges it will provide for self improvement.

Don't try explaining parts of it away. Instead, accept it all and you will experience the freedom that comes when you are free from pride/ego issues.

2. I must be willing to be helped through Biblical teaching.

No matter what excuse we can think up, the truth presented from the instruction of the Bible must be allowed to sink in deep. We must make it our personal habit to ask God to help the Bible speak on a personal level.

3. I must accept Biblical rebuke.

Leaders must see the Bible as important in developing our personal convictions. God wants us to grow and become stronger. Strengthening our convictions is an essential part of growth. This can only happen through rebuke, conviction, admission, repentance, and forgiveness.

4. I must be teachable.

A teachable spirit is a necessity for an effective leader. Learning is a life long endeavor.

5. I must be in training.

Just like an athlete is in training through a strict regiment of exercise and diet, an effective leader is in constant training to become a better leader.

Training regiments vary—but every effective leader has one.

Pride/ego problems don't have to be obstacles to effective leadership. If they are present they need to be removed— the more a leader guards against the obstacle the more effective his/her leadership will be!

QUESTIONS FOR DISCUSSION

1. In what ways is pride/ego disguised in the work place? _____

_____

_____

2. What does it mean to be a "lover of self?" _____

_____

3. Name some of the things included in the checklist of prideful behaviors discussed in this chapter. Share some examples o f t hings y ou h ave s een in l eaders who display these behaviors? _____

_____

_____

4. Have you ever seen anything on the checklist in your own behavior? How did you deal with it/dealing with it? _____

_____

_____

5. How does pride create an attitude of justification?

_____

_____

6. Describe some blind spots created by pride. _____

_____

_____

7. Discuss what the Apostle Paul suggests are some ways to remove the obstacle of pride/ego from the life of the leader. _____

_____

OBSTACLE #11
Security/Insecurity

The final obstacle in our study of effective leadership finishes up the second letter to Timothy from his mentor, Paul. It is a broad picture of life and how it interweaves with other lives for a special plan for each person's life.

These are practical helps for every leader to increase the effectiveness of their leadership endeavors.

This final obstacle to effective leadership plagues many. It is that fine line between insecurity—feeling secure—and feeling too secure. The teaching of the Apostle Paul breaks down this way:

- **Reasons for insecurity**

- **The error of security**

- **How to be spiritually secure**

- **God's security plan**

- **Battling insecurity**

THE REASONS FOR INSECURITY

"In the presence of God and of Christ Jesus, who will judge the living and the dead, and in view of his appearing and

his kingdom, I give you this charge: Preach the Word—be prepared in season and out of season; correct; rebuke; and encourage—with great patience and careful instructions." 2 Timothy 4:1-2

An effective leader does not have to suffer from insecurity. Yet, by virtue of the dynamics of leadership, insecurity is a common problem. The reason is simple: any time you work with people insecurity will be present. It comes from the basic need for affirmation. This need does not get met on a normal basis. It takes a well grounded, balanced person to pull from life the affirmation necessary to not feel insecure once in a while. That type of leader is so rare that it is safe to say everyone becomes insecure from time to time—the key is to catch insecurity before it becomes an obstacle to effective leadership.

Those who are in front of others (for any reason) are the object of criticism. Leaders are always up in front (and will always be criticized). Even the most balanced person can be caught off guard by criticism and the insecurity that follows can become a leadership obstacle.

FIVE WAYS TO PROTECT YOURSELF FROM INSECURITY

1. Stay close to the Bible as your model of development both personally and professionally.

Everyone is insecure by nature because we are born with an emptiness that can only be filled by God. Whenever we feel alone, we get insecure. The Bible helps us stay close to God.

A leader who keeps the Bible at the center of his/her life and career will experience a deep sense of security in God (not security in self).

2. Always be ready—don't make it a habit to lay back.

"In season and out of season" has as its core the inspiration to not become lazy.

Know what you believe and stick with it. Don't get weak in the knees when making decisions because making decisions is part of what leadership is and what leaders do several times on a daily basis.

3. Confront in an effort to settle conflict.

The presentation of "correct" in this passage is the idea of confrontation. Most people hate the thought of confrontation—but clearing the air through confrontation is the best and only way to end the feeling of conflict.

It is much easier to talk about situations when the people involved are not around. Talking in this way is just doing things behind the backs of others. This kind of behavior causes more insecurity for everyone. Insecurity is continually perpetuated in this type of office climate.

The way to remove insecurity from your life is by training yourself to go right up to people—go to the source—to talk, confront, and resolve situations.

4. Make the call—then give yourself the permission to sometimes make a mistake.

Leadership is like being an umpire—you call it safe or out. You don't have the time to consult with anyone or deal with what everyone thinks, or how the call will be taken by all the parties involved.

Leaders should pay attention to people who are actively giving of themselves in your organization. Do not pay attention to the comments coming from the sidelines because the people sitting on the sidelines don't have a clue concerning the pressure you are under.

5.   Encourage others and you will be encouraged.

A leader must build bridges to others. The successful leader does not lay back and force others to reach out.

An effective leader reaches out to everyone who will listen, even the ones who cause the leader to feel insecure. If the effective leader invests in the time, attention and energy necessary, the problems should be solved.

THE ERROR OF SECURITY

"For the time will come when men will not put up with sound doctrine. Instead, to suit their own desires, they will gather around them a great number of people to say what their itching ears want to hear. They will turn their ears away from the truth and turn aside to myths." 2 Timothy 4:3-5

The other extreme of insecurity is a leader who feels too much security. There are always leaders who feel so empowered that they will not listen to the truth. There are those who feel so secure they believe their way of doing things is the only way of doing things. These leaders have had some measure of success in the way they do things that they are now secure in their own success.

There are times when we see leaders who believe they are secure and comfortable. These are three distinct attitudes we see from these secure and comfortable leaders:

- **"I won't do (such and such) because I don't have to do it."**

This is the Apostle Paul's example of "men will not put up with sound doctrine."

- **"I will do whatever suits me and my own desires."**

These are people who have become so secure in their own ways that they readily follow their own thinking with no regard for what any one or any thing thinks.

This clearly illustrates why the Bible is so important. Rather than dismiss the Bible as a book with a bunch of stories, we need to heed it as direction for our lives. When Biblical principles are followed, no one becomes larger or more important than direction given from the Bible.

- **"I will fellowship only with people who agree with me on everything."**

People who feel secure in themselves often portray one of the most insecure behaviors—they only hang out with people who will agree with them.

The Apostle Paul puts it "they will gather around them teachers who will say what their ears itch to hear." What a sad, weak scenario—people who are so insecure that they think they are this secure! The danger Paul relates is gruesome—**"They will turn their ears away from truth and turn aside to myths."** This is the dangerous end to all of those who feel self-secure. The ultimate error is the loss of truth coming into your life— the ultimate tragedy is not being able to recognize truth when it stands before you (which is brought on by self-security).

HOW TO BE SPIRITUALLY SECURE

"But you, keep your head in all situations, endure hardship, do the work of an evangelist, and discharge all the duties of your ministry." 2 Timothy 4:5

As stated before, self-security does as much damage as insecurity.

There is a balance that can be achieved. It involves four specific dimensions.

1. Keep your head in all situations.

Don't b low y our s tack o r lose y our c ool h ead. A n effective leader does not react to criticism or suggestions. Learning to control one's reactions could almost single handedly assure success.

A balanced sense of security helps one keep perspective during all circumstances. Most people aren't impressed with how a leader performs when things are going well, but from how the leader executes when things get tough.

The effectiveness of a leader is proved by how they react during the tough times.

2. Endure hardship.

Hardships will come. It isn't "if" it is "when." Security comes when we can endure our hardships with the help of God. Our dependency on nothing but our faith in God is the key to removing the obstacle of insecurity for effective leadership.

3. Do your work.

There is no substitute for hard work. This notion continues to be repeated when considering the effective leader. When a leader depends on God and works hard, the combination is an unbeatable formula for developing a well balanced feeling of security.

4. Accept responsibility.

Don't try to elude responsibility. Take things head on and get hold of them. Don't be afraid of new responsibilities.

GOD'S SECURITY PLAN

"For I am already being poured out like a drink offering and the time has come for my departure. I have fought the good fight, I have finished the race, and I have kept the faith. Now there is in store for me the crown of righteousness which the Lord, the righteous Judge, will

award to me on that day—and not only to me, but also to all who have longed for his appearing." 2 Timothy 4:6-8

The Apostle Paul knows his life is drawing to a close—that is what gives his writings such an impact. These are things Paul desperately wants to pass on to those he mentors.

It is during a person's final days that we find the best evidence of what a person truly believes and in whom or what he/she places trust.

The idea of "famous last words" always gets our attention. We can see the Apostle Paul characterizes what our lives should be through his closing words of confession.

"I HAVE FOUGHT A GOOD FIGHT"

Paul's confession illustrates his life and leader as a fight—a powerful struggle against an adversary to achieve the prize.

Emotionally speaking, when any leader faces the broad task of leading others, it is a struggle—a fight as Paul puts it. But struggling is what produces God's concept of security with in us. We have to learn to depend on Him to help us with this struggle.

God's plan is that of action. Our struggles are a reminder of that.

"I HAVE FINISHED THE RACE"

The "race" refers to an object or a task. The race can signify any objective or goal set before you. The key to this part of Paul's confession is the idea of completion, execution, conclusion, or discharge.

This illumination that Paul felt was a complete satisfaction in knowing he did his best. God's plan involves us doing our best, and then turning it over to Him.

We should never be satisfied with being mediocre.

"I HAVE KEPT THE FAITH"

A person's faith can involve many ideals--their view of God, their system of worship, and their world view, to name a few.

In this case, Paul is confessing his sense of faithfulness in trusting in God and his conviction of moral truth. He is confessing that he intends to stay faithful for God, the gospel, and his convictions.

Every leader needs a daily personal evaluation in regard to faithfulness. Am I staying steady in my faith? Am I being consistent with what I know as my moral convictions?

By allowing this kind of openness and honesty with yourself —you will see that removing the obstacles to effective leadership is not hard work—and by doing so you will see the impact of your own leadership can have on others and the organization you serve.

The number one need every person has is the need to make a difference—by following Paul's instructions to Timothy—this need can be fulfilled in your life!

QUESTIONS FOR DISCUSSION

1. Discuss the balance between too much security and insecurity in developing effective leadership. _____

   _____

   _____

   _____

2. What are the five ways a leader can protect him/herself from insecurity? _____

   _____

   _____

   _____

   _____

3. Why do people hang out only with people who agree with them? _____

   _____

   _____

   _____

   _____

4. What are the four ways to be spiritually secure? _

   _____

   _____

   _____

   _____

   _____

   _____

5. Explain God's security plan as illustrated by Paul.

   _____

   _____

   _____

   _____

   _____

FINAL THOUGHTS
ON EFFECTIVE LEADERSHIP

"Do your best to come to me quickly, for Demas, because he loved this world, has deserted me and has gone to Thessalonica, Crescens has gone to Galatia, and Titus to Dalmatia. Only Luke is with me. Get Mark and bring him with you, because he is helpful to me in my ministry. I sent Tychicus to Ephesus. When you come bring the cloak that I left with Carpus at Troas, and my scrolls especially the parchments. Alexander the metalworker did me a great deal of harm. The Lord will repay him for what he has done. You too should be on your guard against him, because he strongly opposed our message. At my first defense no one came to my support, but everyone deserted me. May it not be held against them. But the lord stood at my side and gave me strength, so that through me the message might be fully proclaimed and all the Gentiles might hear it. I was delivered from the lion's mouth. The Lord will rescue me from every evil attack and will bring me safely to his heavenly kingdom. To him be glory for ever and ever amen. Greet Priscilla and Aquilla and the household of Onesiphorus—Erastus stayed in Corinth—and I left Trophimus sick in Miletus. Do your best to get here before winter. Eubulus greets you, and so do Pudens, Linust, Claudia and all the brothers. The Lord be with your spirit. Grace be with you." 2 Timothy 4:9-22

In his final words of the letter, Paul lets loose with some startling emotional struggles he has experienced in his leadership. He felt deserted, opposed, and alone. Every leader can identify with Paul.

Every leader feels three things:

- **Deserted from time to time.**

- **Opposed on a regular basis.**

- **Alone most of the time.**

Take these things in stride and don't let them control you emotions—remember if you don't control your own emotions, they will control you.

**"I AM WITH YOU
ALWAYS, EVEN UNTIL
THE END OF TIME."**

--JESUS
